Welcome to Paradise

Other Books

Illustrated Tour of Sacred Places in Hawai'i -
A tour guide to places of special significance.

Hawai'i A Glimpse Into the Past - History of
Hawai'i, told in photos and essays.

Cheap Fun in Hawai'i - How to have a great
Hawaiian vacation without spending a fortune.

49 Things to do on the Big Island - Just what it
sounds like; inexpensive, off-beat things to do
and places to go.

Declare His Praise in the Islands - A history of
Christianity in Hawai'i.

Publish your Book for Free - This is how.

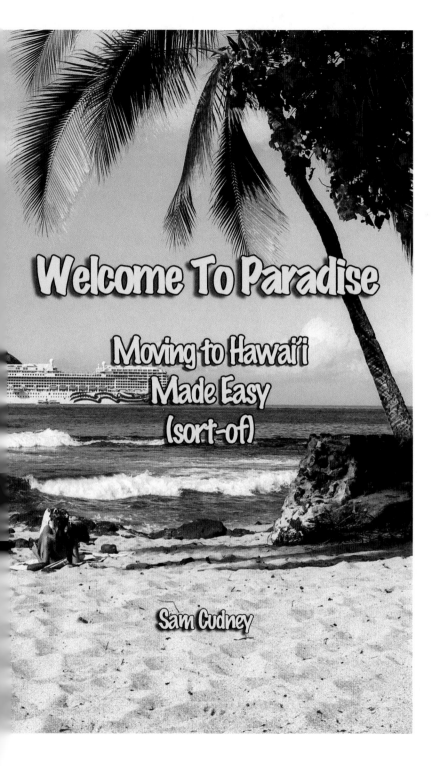

Welcome To Paradise

Moving to Hawai'i
Made Easy
(sort-of)

Sam Cudney

Welcome to Paradise

The opinions are those of the author, his wife, and their cat; the dogs are happy all the time and have no opinion. Any resemblance to persons living or dead is coincidental, except for actual people identified by name. While this is a true and accurate depiction to the best of my knowledge, the author assumes no liability for damages resulting from this book. Don't blame me if you are allergic to pineapple or can't swim or something.

Feel free to e-mail me at *saminhawaii@hotmail.com* if you have any questions or suggestions, I'll try to help. For that matter, feel free to e-mail me just for the fun of it. And sign up for my once-in-a-great-while Mailchimp newsletter; I occasionally give away free books, photos, etc. and Mailchimp is how you'll find out about the freebies. Mailchimp: *http://eepurl.com/URHAD*

And please, please leave a review at Amazon. Reviews are one of the ways Amazon decides when, where, and how to recommend books, so reviews mean I get more books sold, which means I can afford to write more books, which is what I really want to do.

Contents

Introduction

In middle school I was taught to never begin with the phrase "this is a book about..." Flying in the face of that early education, I begin with, this is a book about moving to Hawai'i. If you are thinking about moving to Hawai'i, or think you might think about it, this is for you. Here's our story.

In March of 2012 my wife Amara, our two dogs Bonnie and Bella, Ling the cat, and I moved to Hawai'i's Big Island, the culmination of a long-time dream to have an adventure and to be near water. We thought we were prepared. We had visited this island earlier that year (actually, I had visited all of the islands several times, going back more than a decade), met people and quizzed them about their experiences, bought a house, and read everything we could lay our hands on about the move and about Hawai'i. We planned[1] the move carefully, with checklists and calendars and budgets. We spent months–years, actually–sorting our possessions; friends and charities were on the receiving end of many give-aways.

So much for preparation.

Much of the available information about life in Hawai'i, and moving here, is written by people with a vested interest in the issue (or no knowledge at all) and so presents a picture colored by their perspective. Similarly, visiting as a tourist is a different, more sterile, experience from living as a resident. We knew that, and made an effort to get beneath the veneer of luxury resorts and faux-luau's. Still, we were surprised. This book is intended to help you, the reader and potential future Hawai'i resident, anticipate and deal with many of the surprises we encountered.

If you read no further, remember this: Hawai'i is, in a very practical sense, a foreign country. Dollars are accepted, they speak English, no passports are necessary for US citizens, but moving to Hawai'i is vastly different from moving to San Francisco[2]. Or Fargo, for that matter. Friends and relatives will be many time zones, and perhaps more importantly from a psychological perspective, an ocean away. No one can just "drop in".

---

1   Old saying; if you want to make the Gods laugh, make a plan. Hawaiian deities have a brutal sense of humor.

2   Hawai'i was a kingdom until the overthrow of Queen Lili'uokalani in 1893, and was annexed to the US as a territory in 1898, which goes far to explain why nothing in Hawai'i is named after President McKinley.

And don't plan on frequent visits to the mainland; it's wrenching, as well as being a tedious 5 or 6 hour (minimum) and expensive flight.

The culture here is different, the customs are different, the land is different, the language is different. I'm assuming you have visited, and maybe even stayed for some time. It's not the same. You will not get a true picture of how different until you are immersed in it. We thought we were prepared; we were half right.

We don't regret the move, and would do it again, but we would do some things differently. I began this book as a form of therapy, much like a blog or journal, describing our experiences so that perhaps others could profit from our example. Here is what we learned from our move.

Moving to Hawai'i; the First Steps

So you've decided that you want, or might want, to move to Hawai'i. Good for you! Here are some things to keep in mind.

First, and most important, when it comes to planning, there's no such thing as too far ahead. If you can, start taking serious steps at least a year before you think you might want to move; even earlier is better. I assume you've been here before as a tourist and have some familiarity with Hawai'i, but you will want to visit your "chosen" island or islands at least a couple of times, winter and summer for sure, with the mind set of a potential resident rather than a vacationer. While the climate is pretty much great everywhere, all the time, perfection is in the body temperature of the beholder and what seems great in January while visiting from Minnesota might be a bit on the warm side in July. So, go visit. A lot. How bad can that be, to visit Hawai'i a few times? It's not like you're doing something unpleasant.

There might also be special circumstances such as a job or military transfer that could prevent you from doing much planning or visiting. In that case, you'll just have to go with it, but some planning and research can still help ease the transition. If, for example, your job or military circumstances require you to re-locate to Honolulu or environs, you might not have time for more than a quick visit prior to moving, if any. Keep reading, though; there is still quite a bit that can help you.

While you're here, look around and look beneath the surface, don't just spend your time on the beach (although that's good, too; after all, why move if you can't do what you want?) Visit places where people actually live[3]. Talk with people; your waitress, the guy who rents you a car, the clerk at the grocery store. Tell them you're thinking about moving and be open to their advice. People in Hawai'i are generally more than happy to tell you what a great place it is to live, and how to get the most out of it, as well as what to watch out for. Probably half or more of the people you meet will have moved there from somewhere else (amazingly, or not, ex-Alaskans account for a significant portion of the population). Don't rely too heavily on one person's advice, take it in the aggregate. After a while you'll build a mental

---

3   Some people do actually live in beach-side, resort, condos.

picture of how things work, where to live, and whether or not it will work for you.

My advice to a newcomer is to plan on renting for a while if possible; there is no substitute for living here for a while when it comes to deciding where to live. You might decide that Maui isn't where you want to be, you crave the open spaces of Hawai'i Island or the bustling metropolitan scene of O'ahu. Or, you might decide that the solitude of Hawi isn't for you, you want to be closer to Costco. Be open to the possibility of re-locating.

However, you might have some compelling reason such as pets or about-to-hit capital gains taxes on a home sale to begin home shopping right away. In any event, while you're visiting is a good time to make connections with a real estate person and talk things over with him or her. Naturally, they have some investment in selling you something, but they also have considerable investment in making you happy about it, so they're motivated to give you the straight scoop, albeit with whipped cream, sprinkles, and a cherry on top. They can explain the individual vagaries of their local markets, financing, and the purchase process in general. As is true everywhere else, agents have specialties in terms of areas and housing type, so if you're considering a condo in Waikiki don't look for an agent who specializes in farm land on the Big Island[4]. If the agent sees a mismatch, hopefully he'll tell you and recommend another, probably either a friend or someone in his office, but likely someone more appropriate for your needs.

---

4   For one thing, you can't. One of the peculiarities of Hawai'i real estate is that the multiple listing service (MLS) and agency representations are island-specific; an agent on O'ahu can't work with property on Hawai'i.

Unless that agent is bored and business is awful, they'll not really want to show you homes during these early, fact-finding visits; anything you look at now will be long gone next year when you really plan to move. Instead, they might give you some suggested neighborhoods to look at, maybe a flier or two, and if you're lucky, point you to an open house. If they're at all interested in your business, they'll get your contact information and follow up with you. They might even want to set up a buyer's agent contract, but unless you really feel good about it, you might pass on that; time enough later. Do, though, get on their mailing list.

One way of locating a real estate agent, at least as a starting point, is to ask the agent who is selling your present home. If you are not selling a home, find an agent you like and trust in your area, and ask them for a referral in the area you are planning to relocate to. If all else fails, contact the local Realtor's Association and ask for the names of top-producing agents in your area. They will look within their own companies for the top-producing agents on "your" island. The top-producing agents in Hawai'i are the most likely to have extensive knowledge of housing on the Hawai'i end; plus, they didn't get to be top producing agents by being inept. They may or may not be your final choice, but at least it's a start.

If you plan on renting, the same advice applies. Look at neighborhoods and towns, check with agents and property managers well before moving, if at all possible. If it's to be a fairly sudden re-location, and you are scouting rental housing before re-locating, you can compress the time frame considerably but you'll still need to make some contacts on the Hawai'i end. If nothing else, speak with agents and property managers on the telephone. Do not just show up and hope.

Speaking of listings, you did bring your computer or notebook? Of course you did! You can access the Hawai'i MLS through a number of web sites; the ever-popular *Realtor.com*, *Zillow.com*[5], and links through company web sites such as *Hawaiilife.com*. They all have slightly different search engines, so you will sometimes find something on one site that isn't on another.

Searching the MLS can turn into a fascinating hobby or obsession all its own, one you can take back to the mainland with you. You will begin to see neighborhood and price trends, and get a feel for what agents and companies really move property. In fact, it's very helpful to search out homes that look good on the MLS, then go take a look at them when you're in Hawai'i. This will help you calibrate the sometimes-optimistic MLS descriptions against reality, and give you a much better sense of location. You can even, if you spot something that looks like your dream home, give your agent-friend a call about it, and maybe create an excuse to visit yet again[6].

The actual home buying process in Hawai'i is not significantly different than elsewhere—you give someone money, probably talk nicely with a bank, and they

---

5   This site has a pretty good iPad app, too.

6   Another useful tool is the HGTV channel. In fact, the Real Estate company *Hawai'i Life* has a regular program featuring people shopping for homes in Hawai'i. Beware, though; the TV show is heavily edited.

give you a house and a debt—with a few exceptions. Your bank and the seller's bank will swap a lot of paper, the title company will stand in the middle and charge fees for things you may not quite understand, and at some point, your dream home will be yours. We'll skip over this process because you have probably done it before, and your agent will certainly walk you through it. Besides, it's boring and kind of anticlimactic.

Something to remember is that a lot of the big mainland banks don't have a physical presence in Hawai'i; for example, neither Bank of America nor Wells Fargo, two major mainland lenders, has an office or branch you can visit. The local banks in Hawai'i are small, strong banks with relatively small inventories of bad investments and with lots of cash to lend; plus, you can walk in and talk with a real, live person. They have competitive rates and generally will treat you well[7], although in some ways banking, like many other things, lags the amenities of the mainland by a few years. For example, Bank of Hawai'i just recently added check deposits via smart phone. In retrospect, we probably would have been well served by financing through one of the local banks than through a mainland bank, if only for the personal contact. The rates are competitive, too, although they might be somewhat more conservative than you are used to[8].

Here's a really important thing, whether you're buying a home or renting; absolutely, without fail, have your

---

7   The island thing again. In a small community, there's a very good chance that you'll see the same people again and again.

8   I recently read that more than half of all new residents leave again in 6 months; didn't like it after all, couldn't get a job, etc.

lodging for when you first land, totally locked in. Do not assume you can check in to a motel, there aren't many. I cannot over-emphasize this; casual lodging in Hawai'i is pretty much non-existent.

One thing that you can do that will help both with the house search and with locating a landing place, either temporary or semi-permanent, is to subscribe to the local paper; it's generally available on-line. This falls well into the category of "I wish we'd done that". The local paper is full of ads for condos and apartments for sale or rent (and some are OK with pets); good deals can be had, and they don't show up on the usual vacation rental or real estate web sites. I cannot emphasize this enough; the local paper can be one of your best resources.

It certainly would have helped us. After staying in a really awful place right after landing[9], we moved three times, finally finding a pet-friendly condo with a very reasonable monthly rental rate located close to our eventual house, in the local paper. By all means, get the local paper. Besides, it gives you a feel for the flavor of the place that you can't get any other way. For example, our newspaper here in Kailua-Kona, *West Hawai'i Today*[10], frequently has front-page, above-the-fold, articles about local school activities. Even the TV news histrionics are likely to be about a new sewer line or broken water main. We are aware of national and international news and politics, perhaps even more so than many mainland residents because of the cosmopolitan nature of the

---

9   Because of the dogs and cat, we were limited in housing choices.

10   Available on-line; an invaluable resource in house- and temporary quarters hunting.

population, but it just doesn't matter all that much on a day-to-day basis. The second page always features a large color photograph by a local person of some local beauty spot. New York Times it isn't, but we're not in New York.

While you're making one of those before-the-move visits, rent a mailbox at one of those mailbox/packing places[11] as a temporary forwarding address. You'll need a safe, sure-fire address for forwarded mail, and some things, like magazines, require a really long time to catch up. Unless you just can't live without seeing the latest issue of *Bagpipe Monthly* hot off the press, do that right away so you can start forwarding well before the actual move. Imagine your joy when you go to your mailbox and find things addressed to you, in Hawai'i! And think how nice it will be to have that Hawai'i address to keep you going; there will be times when you will need it.

But what about the move itself? Pretty much all household goods will be transported by sea. You can rent a container from, for instance, a company like PODS, or work with a moving company to move you[12]. It is expensive; we paid said moving company $1.67 a pound to have our goods packed, shipped, and unpacked. You will want to make arrangements at least a couple of months in advance, and plan on 2 to 4 weeks, or more, for your goods to be in transit.

---

11   These places will tell you over the phone whether or not you have mail waiting, accept packages, and re-forward things. Much more flexible than the post office.

12   If you don't have a lot of possessions, you can mail things, which is cheap but annoying. It can be a long time before you see your packages. Some people take this route.

You will also want to carefully weigh (ha!) what you take. You probably will not need that down quilt, but if it makes you happy, take it; just accept that it may stay in its box forever. Leave the snowblower behind, too (but bring the snow shovel, it's a great dustpan); sell it for what you can get. Furniture is heavy and moving costs will be based in part or whole on weight, and Hawaiian houses are generally smaller, so you may not need all of your furniture. Sort things mercilessly, have yard sales, donate generously to charity, and really, really organize your stuff, or moving will be miserable. This way, the misery is spread out.

This is an agonizing process. In a "normal" move you can kind of ignore some of the flotsam and jetsam you've collected, either by quickly stuffing it in a box and making a mental promise to get to it later (ha! As if…), or by telling the moving guys "everything in that closet" and letting them stuff it in boxes for you. If nothing else, the sheer expense of moving to Hawai'i forces you to look at each and every item and make a decision about its value to you. It brought us face to face with a lot of issues. For example, do we really need artwork by a friend's 7-year-old? How often, and to where, will we visit the mainland, and what clothing should we take along for that purpose? How many refrigerator magnets do we really need? Will that sheepskin rug look good with a layer of beach sand? Do we really have room in the new home?

Do take work- and business-related things, electronics, tools, kitchen things. These are universal and if you need it on the mainland you will probably need it in

Hawai'i. It will probably be cheaper to bring it than to replace it. Consider carefully things that are local or seasonal. Bring anything related to water sports, bicycling, fishing, hiking, etc. The moving company will not accept things like paint and garden chemicals, so give them away or take them to your local household hazardous waste facility. Firearms[13] are a problem, you need permits and things in Hawai'i, so research this carefully; there is some game hunting, but in general, there are not many firearms and very specific laws about importing them[14]. In brief, consider the cost of replacing each item, new, vs the cost of taking it. Some things will be replaceable from yard sales, but don't count on it.

Don't ship anything you will need during the transition period; medicines, prescriptions, identification, important paperwork such as your passport and social security card, should all travel with you. This is very important. Obvious, but sometimes we forget. Do be sure and have enough clothing, etc for the weeks or months that you and/or your goods are in transit. You will need things.

Bring cash! Chances are good that your bank doesn't do business in Hawai'i, so opening a bank account with a local bank with a check on your mainland bank is a

---

13 A lawyer friend told me that Hawai'i is the anti-Florida; there is no "castle" defense, and no "stand your ground". If threatened, you have an obligation to run away and avoid conflict. Hawai'i ranks # 43 in the nation in violent crimes per capita; Florida is number 2. I guess there is something to "run away and avoid conflict". Source; http://www.statemaster.com/graph/cri_vio_cri-crime-violent

14 You have 15 days to declare and register imported firearms. Other laws apply as well. Stringent ones.

good idea, but you'll still need some cash while your check clears (which can take up to 10 business days). You can transfer money from your mainland bank via ACH transfer (cheap but slow) or wire transfer (fast and expensive), but there's no substitute for paper money. Some businesses simply don't accept credit cards. You can always, of course, visit the ATM and pay the out-of-network fee, but there isn't an ATM on every corner. In fact, they can be few and far between.

Don't forget to tell your friends on the mainland about time zones; Hawai'i is 3 hours behind the west coast, and 6 behind the east coast, during mainland daylight savings time[15]. So, when cousin Esmeralda in Pittsburgh calls you at 10 am her time, it's 4 in the morning Hawai'i time. This will happen. A lot. Leave your phone in another room with the ringer turned off when you go to bed. After a while, they'll catch on.

Start forwarding your mail to your rented box in Hawai'i a week or two before you leave. It is amazing how many addresses you will need to change eventually, so don't panic yet, you'll catch them later and this way, nothing important gets overlooked. The post office is pretty good about forwarding, and for $15/week or so will even forward mail via priority mail (a good idea) rather than standard. The regular change-of-address forwarding is good for a year, so you have time to get organized. You can handle the forwarding on-line, just do a permanent change of address via the post office

---

15 Hawai'i does not observe daylight savings time because it would be pointless. Being so close to the equator, winter and summer days are nearly the same length year 'round.

to the rented box address, don't bother making permanent changes with your bank, credit card company, Aunt Millie, etc yet until you have a permanent address. This should hold you for a year. Once you're settled in to your new home, you can change the forwarding address with the post office yet again, and start changing all those addresses you've accumulated over the years. It seems like a little more work, but it takes the uncertainty out of the process.

Basically, think of the move as a three-step process;

- You pack up your stuff and vacate your old house,
- You stay in temporary lodging on the mainland, in Hawai'i, or both, and
- You move in to your longer-term housing in Hawai'i.

There are a lot of variables in this process; you might have bought a home in Hawai'i on one of your visits and have it all outfitted and ready to go, in which case you aren't reading this chapter anyway. You might be military personnel or have short-or long-term company housing available. Or, you might plan on staying in a rental home for a few weeks or months while house-hunting, or you might even be planning on changing islands from time to time while you look for the perfect place. The key is that it's a long trip; you are not likely to leave your home on the mainland, get on an airplane, get off the airplane and move in to your new home all ready to go. There will be a period in which your goods are unavailable and you are essentially homeless.

We have friends who took the rent-while-looking approach. They, unlike us, rented a condo for (initially) 3 months, then on a month-to-month basis while they house-shopped. Ten months later, they are finally in their new home. In effect, they have been living out of suitcases during that entire period. If this seems hard to you, it's because it is. It is not an easy move.

Vehicles are another story, and chapter. You can ship your car, it costs about $1100, plus the cost of getting it to the shipping terminal (San Diego, LA, San Francisco, Seattle) and takes 3 weeks or so. A motorcycle costs about the same as a car to ship, surprisingly, and depending on the shipper, you might not be able to smuggle your motorcycle into the shipping container that has your household goods. In fact, you can't ship the car full of stuff, either[16]. It has to be empty and clean for agricultural inspection; they don't want invasive species such as weed seeds coming in with a muddy car.

Moving to Hawai'i is a bigger deal than moving to a contiguous state; it's more like moving to another country except that you don't need a passport or different currency. Ideally, you can plan on a year's preparation time, a month or two of actually getting ready, and at least a month of transition during which your goods and you are in transit. Worth it? We think so.

---

16 Unless you've rented a 40 ft container and packed it with car, household goods, and everything else. Some people do that. There are lots of ways to make the actual move. Research!

So you want to bring Woofy (or Fluffy) to Hawai'i?

This is so important and so complicated that we're giving it an entire chapter to itself. If you still want to bring pets after reading this, well, you really love them. Let's find out.

There are two main problems with bringing pets from the mainland to Hawai'i;

- Hawaiian pet import procedures are arduous, and
- Hawai'i is not especially pet-friendly.

Hawai'i is a unique, and fragile, ecosystem. The native species have evolved without the competitors, predators, and diseases found on the mainland. There are no snakes and no rabies in Hawai'i, and the Hawai'i Department of Agriculture means to keep it that way. You can only bring domestic dogs, cats, and horses (no snakes, lizards, birds, fish, wolf-hybrids, or other common and not-so-common pets) to Hawai'i, and only then after complying with a stringent set of rules. To make the process even more arduous, the physical act of bring your pet(s) is pretty forbidding. For one thing, they may be quarantined on arrival; the only exceptions are service animals and pets from the UK, Australia, New Zealand, and Guam, and even then there are some pretty specific requirements.

On the good side, the quarantine period can be a short as a few minutes, if you've followed all the rules. It can also be 120 days, or even outright refusal to enter, if you haven't. Hawai'i's "5 days or less" quarantine program, which can include direct release of Woofy or Fluffy to you at the airport, is what you want to shoot for. Here's how it works[17].

- To qualify, dogs and cats must have had two documented rabies vaccinations, at least 30 days apart, with the most recent at least 90 days prior to arrival in Hawai'i.

- They must have had a specific blood test, called a FAVN test, performed by a specific laboratory, no

---

17 A summary only; so check with Hawai'i Department of Agriculture at their website -- http://hawaii.gov/hdoa/ai/aqs/aqsbrochure.pdf .There are also checklists, and a lot of general guidance on the Department of Agriculture website.

less than 120 days before arrival. This requirement is probably the critical path. That's about another $100 per pet for the analysis, plus the cost of your vet drawing the blood and shipping the sample FedEx earliest next day delivery. Results will be sent directly to the Hawai'i Department of Agriculture. The Department of Agriculture has a website that lists the FAVN results[18], collated by microchip number, which is how they identify pets. Woofy will forever be 13E25AAB252 to them. Woofy does have a microchip, doesn't he?

- You must send the completed, notarized import forms (http:// Hawai'i.gov/hdoa/ai/aqs/AQS-278.pdf), with *original* rabies vaccination certificates for the last two vaccinations, to the Department of Agriculture, along with a money order or cashier's check for a pretty hefty sum, prior to arrival. If you will be flying to Honolulu, the forms must be sent at least 10 days in advance. If you are flying to Maui, the Big Island, or Kaua'i (called the Neighbor Islands), the forms must be sent at least 30 days prior. The fee ranges from $145 to $224 per pet, depending on where you plan to land[19]. The forms are pretty much self-explanatory. You will need to identify your arrival date and flight on the form, so now is a good time to contact the airline and make flight arrangements. Actually, it's better to have done that much earlier; shipping an animal is not the same as sending Uncle Fred a souvenir Aloha shirt.

---

18   http://hawaii.gov/hdoa/ai/aqs/aqs-microchip6-11.pdf

19   And it generally has to be a direct flight from the mainland, if you're going to one of the neighbor islands; no stopping in Honolulu first, unless that's your destination.

• It's a good idea to include a self-addressed, stamped, priority- or express-mail envelope with your submittal; otherwise, it can take a couple of weeks for the documentation to reach you. In fact, it will take a while anyway, so do all this as early in the process as you can; as soon as you have ticket reservations.

• Upon receipt and approval, the Department of Agriculture will send you two documents for each pet; a bright yellow sticker for the kennel that directs airline personal to deliver the pet to the quarantine area, and a blue-bordered form that gives you specific permission to bring your pet. You must keep that form with you when you fly, as you will be asked for it at least twice.

• If the Department of Agriculture finds a problem with your documentation, they will contact you. They are very nice people and do not wish you any ill, they simply want to keep Hawai'i rabies free (hence the name of their web domain, www.rabiesfree Hawai'i.gov Makes the point, doesn't it?) They cannot, however, waive any of the requirements.

• For direct release at a neighbor island (that means, you get off the plane on Maui, Kaua'i, or Hawai'i Island and collect Woofy right away. This is what you want), you must contract in advance with an approved veterinary clinic at the destination for an arrival health check. Guess what! This also costs money. Quite a bit, actually; plan on about $135 per pet, arranged and paid in advance. The Department of Agriculture maintains a list of approved veterinarians on each neighbor island. If you're flying to Honolulu, the Department of Agriculture will handle this inspection, and you've paid for it already, so it's simpler.

- No more than 14 days before departure, you must have the animals inspected yet again by a veterinarian, and flea and tick treatment containing Fipronil (example, Frontline) applied. The vet will provide yet another health certificate, which again identifies the rabies vaccinations and specifically states that the animals have been treated with Fipronil. Try and find a vet who has prepared animals for Hawai'i, as it's not good to be the only expert in the room. **Important!** Since the airlines will also want a health check and certificate (typically no more than 10 days prior to departure), you should probably do this penultimate examination at the same time as the Fipronil treatment. There goes another $100 per pet.

That's the up-front preparation. It is a good idea to establish a calendar with the various pet-related dates, starting backwards from your intended landing date. Since the time intervals are all critical and relatively inflexible, and some are pretty short, you don't want to take a chance on missing something. The calendar sure saved us from a few potential boo-boos. There is a basic calendar attached at the end of this book that includes the critical pet dates, but you should probably transfer the advance dates to your own calendar.

Now, it's time to talk about flying. Each airline has its own policies, but they all pretty much require the same general things. Woofy must travel in an appropriate kennel, with food and water dishes and various labels. Be careful here; some airlines are very specific about kennel dimensions and details, and the people at the chain pet supply store will not know them. Just because the kennel says it's "airline approved" doesn't mean it is. For example, United and Alaska Airlines both are very specific about kennel construction, requiring a 1" lip around the kennel and screwed-together assembly, no snaps. On the good news side of things, the airline will probably supply labels and documentation, but check first. And since animal transport is out of the ordinary for the airline, make your reservations as early as you can, and keep checking back to be sure they know about the pets; this information can get lost in their process. Press for confirmation numbers for each of your pets, or you could be in for an unpleasant surprise at the airport.

Some airlines will only accept one animal, others will accept more. Most limit the total number on a flight. None will let a pet travel as cabin baggage[20] to Hawai'i due to the quarantine regulations, so Fluffy stays in the hold. Most have special counters or receiving areas for pets[21]. For example, United/Continental's *Petsafe* program, which has an excellent safety record, generally requires that the pet be dropped off at the air freight terminal no more than 4

---

20 Exception; bona-fide service animals.

21 Strangely, when we did it, animals and military personal were directed to the same United Airlines counter at LAX. We felt very sorry for the non-animal people in the very long line behind us.

24

hours, and at least 2 hours, prior to flight time, yet another thing to deal with. If your flight has a transfer before leaving the mainland, you may have to supply food with the pet. You will have to provide documentation about when the pet was last fed and watered, and when it is next due (the airline may well have their own forms; check beforehand). You will be asked for the Hawai'i Department of Agriculture import authorization forms and the veterinarian's health certificate at check-in time. The airline will make copies and give you back the originals.

The airline will also ask for a healthy sum of money, too. Be prepared to shell out something in the $400–$1000 range, per pet, for flights out of the west coast.

The kennels will be inspected by TSA at the departure point, so bring leashes and collars in your carry-ons because the TSA agent most definitely will not stick his hand in an occupied kennel. Once inspected, labeled, tagged, and documented, Woofy will be whisked away to a holding area, then stashed aboard your plane. You can stop worrying at this point, at least for a while. Animals are held in a temperature-controlled area at the airport and loaded last; some airlines will not transport animals if the forecast is above or below threshold temperatures at the points of departure and arrival, or stops in between.

Don't worry about the actual flight. With a few exceptions (and statistics are available on-line), airlines have an excellent safety record for transporting animals. Once they turn out the lights, the animals get to nap in air-conditioned, pressurized comfort, uninterrupted by vapid movies and kicking children. They also have more leg room than you do.

A nice touch, by the way, is United Airline's policy of leaving a little "I'm safely aboard" card on your seat, informing you that Woofy is indeed in the hold. This is very comforting.

On arrival, either at Honolulu International Airport or a neighbor island airport, the animals will be unloaded immediately and taken to the quarantine area where either your contracted veterinarian or the Department of Agriculture vet will examine them yet again. When you go to collect them, you will be asked for the original examination certificate from the mainland 14 days ago and the import authorization forms (you did put those in your carry-on, didn't you?), and will fill out yet another form. Then and only then, if everything is OK, will Woofy be released to you care. Or rather, Woofy in his kennel; the rules specify that the animal must remain in the kennel until they are removed from the quarantine area (note; it's Hawai'i, after all; your particular vet/quarantine agent/baggage services agent may not be a stickler for this most trivial of rules, but be prepared to move Woofy, in his box, to your rental car).

Conveniently, the airport will have a designated area for Woofy to relieve himself after spending 8 hours or so in his kennel (Hawaiian destinations are 5 or 6 hours flying time from west coast airports, so Woofy has had a lot of kennel time). You will need a poop bag, also usually supplied at the "relief" area.

Now, you're in Hawai'i. What next?

Well, you had better have already locked in your lodgings well in advance. There are not a lot of "casual" motels in Hawai'i (generally speaking, none, so don't bother looking for a Motel 6), many resorts and vacation rentals do not accept pets, and those that do, want only one small pet. If you show up with your team of Huskies and expect to just drop in at the Marriott, you're going to be unpleasantly surprised, not to mention homeless.

In fact, the surprise may even start at the airport; Enterprise, for one, won't allow animals in their cars (some flimsy excuse about potential customer allergies which, if true, would mean that we'd see rental cars hurtling off the road at a record pace. The truth is that they don't want to spend the time cleaning. Heck, the rental contract even specifies "no sand". It's Hawai'i; can you imagine "no sand"?)

So, have your lodgings sorted out first. If I keep saying this, it's because it's very important. If you have already bought and closed on a home, have the address and key with you. If there is a deal pending, don't assume you'll close on it that afternoon and move in later the same day. If you're staying with friends for a while, life will be a little easier since they are expecting you and Woofy (you did tell them, didn't you?)

If, like us, you arrive before your permanent lodgings are secure and are staying in temporary quarters, be prepared to have Woofy in your company 24/7, and to be ostracized from many of the activities people go to Hawai'i for. There are no dog beaches (well, one, but it's a secret and will remain so as far as I'm concerned. Look me up when you get here and I'll reveal it), no dog parks, no dog-friendly restaurants... the list goes on. Lots of people in Hawai'i have dogs, but none of the visitors do, and the economy and infrastructure is geared for the visitors. People who live and work here leave the dogs at home when they go shopping/to work/out to eat/to the beach. You'll be doing that, too.

That's not to say they hate animals; to the contrary, there is an active "catch/neuter/release" program for the zillions of feral cats, and, realistically, would they go to all this trouble if they just hated animals, and Woofy in particular? It'd be simpler to just prohibit animal imports and let the dog and cat population die out. They simply separate the economic engine, tourism, from their enthusiasm for animals. Not all tourists want Woofy to slobber on them. You will find as you walk down the street with Woofy on his leash and poop bag in your pocket[22] that a sizeable percentage of tourists will stop to pet your pet, so to speak, and talk about their little Fudgie back home. Unless Woofy has a taste for stranger's legs (in which case, you might re-think this plan), humor them. You got to bring your best friend with you.

---

22 Very important to have! Here's a hint; those plastic bags that grocery stores use for produce make dandy poop bags, just be careful if you have long fingernails, and don't wave it around too much, the bags are generally flimsy.

The Big Island

This is where we live, so I'll have the most to say about it. The "proper" name is Hawai'i, or Hawai'i Island, but that's too confusing (after all, many people don't even know there's more than one island) so even locals call it Big Island because it is, well, big. Bigger than all the other islands in the state put together, in fact[23].

Each island has its own culture, its own "feel". Kaua'i is a lush garden, Maui is lively, O'ahu is urban and sophisticated, and Hawai'i is rural. The other main islands – Kaho'lawae, Lana'i, Moloka'i, and Ni'ihau, are

---

23 At 4028 square miles, more or less, it's slightly smaller than Connecticut. Not as crowded, though.

uninhabited, sparsely inhabited, or privately owned. It has a bit of "old west" feel in places. It also has a "jungle" feel, an "old Hawai'i" feel, a "tourist mecca" feel, a "Rocky Mountain" feel, an "arctic tundra" feel, a "desert" feel, an "ohmyGod this must be what hell looks like" feel, a "beach" feel, and a few dozen others. There's even a "back side of the moon" feel to some of the fresher lava flows. And that's one of the distinguishing features of the Big Island; it's diverse.

Depending on who you talk to and how knowledgeable they really are, the Big Island has 17 of the world's 18 climate zones, or 52 of the 53, or whatever. In the most widely-used system, the Koppen system, the Big Island has 4 of the 5 major zones, and 8 of the 13 sub zones[24]. That's pretty good; after all, there's no trophy for having the most climate zones. You can pretty much pick your temperature and rainfall.

Like the other islands, most of the development is along the coast, with the sunny-beachy resorts on the west, or dryer, coast, and the older, damper (and lusher) parts on the east, or wetter, coast. Kilauea, the most currently-active volcano, didn't pay attention to any of this and decided to locate at the southern end of the island. It didn't have a choice, really; Hawai'i is on a part of the Pacific crustal plate that's slowly traveling northwest, and the islands are where a thin spot allows magma from the earth's interior to leak through, making islands. The magma leak stays put and the plate

---

24 Missing are continental winter dry, continental summer dry, polar ice cap, continental continuously wet, and temperate winter dry. I don't know what some of those are.

slides over it, resulting in a long, skinny chain of islands. We're not talking NASCAR speeds here; it's about 8 cm a year[25].

Hawai'i Island being on the southeast-most end of the chain, is the newest, and is composed of 5 volcanoes, one of which, Kilauea, is busy making more land[26] while two others are considered "active". This relative newness accounts for a lot of the physical character of the island. The mountains are bigger[27], the newer lava flows haven't had a chance to break down into soil, rivers haven't really formed, the beaches are small and young, etc. It's also partly responsible for the size of the island; it hasn't had a chance to erode away much, either.

Much of the western and southern parts of the island are visible lava flows; deep black for the more recent ones, and reddish-brown for the older flows. The bones of the earth are very visible here. Think "*Jornada del Muerte*" in the continental southwest, only rougher. The northern and eastern areas, where the lava has had a chance to decay into soil and where rainfall is plentiful are lush and green, is somewhat like coastal Oregon, only warm. Inland on both sides, and up the slopes a bit, things are greener than on the coast.

The lava is the dominant feature over a good-sized portion of the western part of the island. It is unrelentingly black and rough, with some scruffy vegetation and

---

25 Although in geologic terms, this is pretty snappy.

26 In fact, in some places you can stand on land younger than you are.

27 Mauna Kea is the tallest mountain on earth, if you start counting at its base, which is under about 20,000 ft of water. It's 33,500 ft tall, of which the top 13,500 or so sticks out of the Pacific.

equally scruffy goats[28] scattered here and there, except when it rains, when the black lava suddenly is covered with a layer of green vegetation, seemingly out of nowhere. Locals and visitors have found a unique way to decorate it; nowhere but on Hawai'i Island do you find graffiti done in bleached coral against the black lava. Sentiments like *"Bob loves La'i"* and *"Aloha"* and *"Class of '11"* abound. Being bleached coral against black lava, it's pretty visible. A debate rages as to whether this is vandalism, or just a continuation of native Hawaiian art forms. Some do-gooders take it on themselves to collect the coral and "clean up" the lava, but that seems a Sisyphusan effort. Most people don't care; a typical attitude towards about everything except maybe the ocean. Frankly, considering the effort involved, I'm impressed that anyone bothers with either the coral writing or the clean-up.

The land is steep; the slope of the island is clearly visible looking parallel to the coast, and it's nothing to climb or drop a few thousand feet in elevation going from place to place. Going from Kailua-Kona to Hilo involves a climb from sea level to 6500 ft and back down to sea level over a distance of maybe 50 miles. Grades of 15% to 18% are not unheard-of, and it's a 25% average grade down into the Waipeo Valley and on part of the road up to the visitor center on Mauna Kea. The Big Island is hard on car brakes.

The night sky is stunning; the air is clear (most of the time) and the stars are bright. The Milky Way is

---

28 Black and brown Spanish Goats abound; British sailing ships dropped off goats wherever they made landfall on islands so there'd be a food source for the next ship by. Although goat as a dietary staple seems to have faded away from cruise ship menus, the goats are still here.

clearly visible, and identifying constellations takes on new dimensions because there are so many stars[29]. At a latitude of about 20 North, portions of the southern sky not ordinarily visible to observers in the continental US can be seen; including, barely, the Southern Cross. In fact, we just learned that the very slight elevation of the Southern Cross above the horizon was a navigational aid for Polynesian voyagers to tell when they had reached the latitude of Hawai'i.

A side note about the night sky; street lights in towns near Mauna Kea use those horrid sodium vapor lights, with heavy shielding over the tops. This is because the sodium vapor light can be easily filtered out of the light collected by the telescopes on Mauna Kea. It's kind of a *kokua*[30] for astronomers.

About that clear air; due to the presence of a volcano that's been continuously erupting since the mid-80's, we sometimes have quite a bit of sulfur dioxide and particulates in the air, depending on where you are and how the wind is blowing. When the trade winds drop off, the volcanic fog, or vog, forms a layer of cruddy air that makes the sky a bit grey and is generally unattractive. Despite this, people in Hawai'i have the longest lifespan of any state, by quite a margin, so clearly, there's more to longevity than air pollution.

Beaches on the Big Island might not be what you expect; they are not endless miles of flat, white sand, like

---

29 Which goes a long way towards explaining the presence of a dozen major observatories, including the twin Keck telescopes, the largest in the world, on Mauna Kea.

30 Hawaiian word meaning to extend help to another or cooperate, not for personal gain.

Florida. Beaches are relatively small and separated by areas of lava, sometimes very steep areas. Actually, this is generally true for beaches anywhere in Hawai'i. Despite this, some of the Hawaiian beaches, including Hapuna on the west side of the Island, always make everybody's list of the best beaches in the world.

The sand is generally a little coarse, not the very fine stuff found on the mainland, might not be white (black and green are two possibilities), and there are relatively few shells. Again, this is because the beaches are relatively new, in geologic terms. Unlike Florida and parts of California, you can't drive on the beaches. First, because it's illegal; it's dangerous to other beach users. And second, where would you go? In fact, you can't even have kayaks or canoes on some of the more crowded[31] beaches because of potential dangers to others.

The more popular beaches on the Big Island are on the west side because it's sunnier and that's where all the tourist resorts are. The shoreline is state property, so even the snootiest resort areas have to allow public access (although some of them have found ways to limit parking, which is reasonable). Locals can mingle freely with $1000/day visitors, and if no one's complaining, even use the beach chairs. One nice touch; most beaches have warm, fresh water showers to rinse off the salt.

Which by way of a segue, brings us to visitors and locals. The total resident population of Hawai'i Island is about 180,000, out of a state population of about

---

31   A relative term; at the peak of visitor season, on the most crowded day,
        it's still possible to have a private conversation pretty much anywhere.

1,300,000. Added to that, on average, every 5th person on the Big Island is a visitor. That's a lot of visitors.

The population of Kailua-Kona, the main center of everything on the west side of the Island, is about 12,000. It's a safe bet that sooner or later you'll see people you know at the grocery store or Costco. Everybody has a passing familiarity with just about everybody else. Thus, an unfamiliar face is almost certain to be a visitor. Further cementing this assumption will be skin that's either laser red with sunburn or moonlight white; residents tend towards various shades ranging from medium oak to deep mahogany, and a few develop skin like goat leather, which is generally not attractive in female persons. If they're wearing socks, or something matches something else, they're probably a visitor. So, at the beach, "where are you from?" is generally the first question to a stranger. Actually, everywhere; not just at the beach.

Visitors are pretty much welcomed everywhere, and not just because they bring dollars or yen. It's a part of the Hawaiian culture that is deeply ingrained. My theory is that it's a consequence of being an island culture without a nearby continent to fall back upon[32]. On a small island where everybody knows everybody (remember Kailua-Kona has only 12,000 people), it's essential to get along. People in Hawai'i really, really need each other. And really, really work at it.

This manifests in some interesting ways. For one obvious "it's not Florida!" fact, guns are rare. Handguns

---

32 There is good evidence that Polynesian or Hawaiian navigators "discovered" America a good 400 years before Columbus. However, seeing that it was already occupied and a going affair, they apparently decided to be polite and leave it alone.

are practically non-existent, and the gun laws make it a serious crime to possess a gun, much less use it, without proper registration, etc. So aside from sport and food hunters, there're no guns. There's not even the possibility of "concealed carry"; just not going to happen. Amazingly, the crime rate is low. So much for those theories about armed citizens.

Oh, things do happen, generally fueled by alcohol and drug use, although that's not as common as you'd think. And nobody gets shot. Some theft now and then, the occasional drunken argument that involves sharp objects, but no mass murders, no husband-wife shoot outs, no over-zealous neighborhood watches. In fact, we marvel that the newspaper has anything to report. Much of the front page of the Kailua-Kona newspaper, *West Hawai'i Today*, is devoted to community activities. The *Honolulu Star Advertiser* is a different story. Being a real city, they tend to have a bit more excitement, but often the news is things like a broken water main or high surf.

We do have a Driving Under the Influence (DUI) problem; about 20 people a month are arrested for DUI. They are nearly always sentenced to fines ranging from $500 up, court-ordered referral to treatment programs, blow 'n' go breath analyzers in their cars, and for second offenders, jail terms (not movie star overnight terms, either). Courts are serious about this[33].

Is society in Hawai'i tightly regulated? Yes it is. No guns, mandatory annual vehicle inspection, stringent

---

33 Also serious about using your cell phone while driving. It's a $300 fine for a first offense.

zoning laws (I read in the paper that a landowner was recently fined in the 6 digits for building too close to the shore, and ordered to remove the offending construction, his house), and heavily protected cultural sites (road construction can take decades while the cultural significance of a route is discussed). You can't import many animals or plants; as we've seen, you can't even bring your dog without jumping through a lot of hoops. Speed limits are zealously enforced; you might get away with 5 mph on the highway, but not 10, and never in a school zone. There is good news about this, though; minor traffic offenses have been de-criminalized and there is no "point" system for speeds up to 19 mph over the limit, just a fine.

It's similar to Northern and Western Europe in a way; the citizens have agreed on, and accepted, a somewhat higher level of regulation than, say, Texas, in return for a higher level of security. We can walk down a dark street without fear, door locks are optional in many places, and children are safe from predators.

It does seem to work. Let's compare Hawai'i with two other self-proclaimed paradises, North Korea and Florida. Consider the following:

Quality of Life Score

	Hawai'i	N. Korea	Florida
Hula dancing	Yes	No	No
Great snorkeling, surfing	Yes	No	Yes
Nat'l Geographic World's top beaches	Yes	No	Yes
Unlikely to be shot	Yes	No	No
Loco Moco	Yes	No	No
Timely election results	Yes	Yes	No
Great weather	Yes	No	Yes
Ukelele music everywhere	Yes	No	No
Birthplace of Don Ho	Yes	No	No
Great coffee	Yes	No	No
Totals	**10**	**1**	**3**

As you can see, based on these important parameters, Hawai'i is clearly a nicer place to live than either North Korea or Florida. Especially the Big Island.

More on Housing in Hawai'i

Yes, there are normal houses in Hawai'i. If your only experience with this tropical paradise it a 10 day stay at a luxury resort, you might not realize this fact. Of course, you might not need to know it; it's entirely possible to live in a resort complex on a permanent basis, but that's only one of the possibilities.

Generally speaking, there are fewer categories of long-term, permanent housing in Hawai'i than on the mainland. They are;

- Owning or renting a condo,
- Renting an apartment,
- Owning or renting a house.

There are no trailer parks, no RV parks, no temporary-by-design-but-permanent-in-practice housing[34], no by-the-week motels. The reasons for this are complex and probably the basis of many a dissertation, but basically, it's because the permanent population is mostly permanent. These are islands, much smaller than continents, and people pretty much stay in one place. There's no visiting-this-place-and-going-to-that-place that the more mobile residents of North America seem to enjoy. Add to that the islanders' emphasis on family and community (again, enhanced by the fact that these are islands), and the further factor that everything pretty much is imported so there aren't any cheap rusty old trailers, and certainly a few other considerations, and we have a pretty limited set of housing options.

It goes without saying that real estate, like about everything else in Hawai'i, is expensive. We're not talking Tokyo prices, but it's not Detroit, either. Right now, housing prices are still down from the housing crisis, but rising. It's on a par with, say, good California coast property. At this writing, $400,000 will get you a 350 sq ft condo on the 12th floor of a Honolulu high rise, or a 1300 sq ft home with a yard in a bedroom community outside of Kailua Kona. The same money will get you a whole block in a distressed area such as parts of Central Florida, or a modest home in San Luis Obispo, or nothing at all in Beverly Hills. Expensive, in other words, if you're used to Midwest prices, but not out of line with California.

---

34   There are a few hearty souls and homeless people who camp on the beach or live in their car, but not many.

Here's something about owning a house in Hawai'i that often goes unnoticed. If it's your primary residence, you're entitled to a break on property taxes. On Hawai'i Island the minimum amount of the break is $40,000, increasing to $80,000 if you're between the ages of 60 and 69. There's also an additional exemption of 20% of the value up to $80,000. It varies from island to island and year to year; on Maui, for example, the base exemption for home owners is $160,000. This is a pretty good break on property taxes.

There's an old saying about real estate – location, location, location – and Hawai'i is no exception. Conveniently, there are three main location factors in Hawai'i;

- Which island?
- How far from the beach?
- Which town/climatic area?

To recap, Hawai'i as a state consists of 4 populated islands; Kaua'i, O'ahu, Maui, and Hawai'i. Each has its own flavor and desirability as a place to live.

Kaua'i is the smallest, and the farthest north. It has a very small population, and thus fewer services. Housing is about second-cheapest, because it's absolutely gorgeous but pretty rural.

O'ahu is the next in line, moving south. It's the most populated, and generally the most expensive. Honolulu, the state capital, is the most densely populated state capital in the US in terms of percentage of state population living in the capital. There is a strong military presence on O'ahu, which helps keep housing prices down a bit in some areas. If you have or need a job that's not in the service industry, or need serious medical attention, then O'ahu is the logical choice.

Maui is next south. It's expensive, a match for O'ahu. It is arguably more tourist-y than the other islands, with the exception of the Waikiki area of Honolulu.

Hawai'i, the Big Island, is farthest south. It's the least expensive. It's very rural, and sparsely populated. One potential issue with Hawai'i Island is the presence of a very active volcano, and attendant air pollution.

Distance from the beach has a big effect on property value (as does the view, but that's not quite as big a factor). If you want to be easy walking distance to white, sandy beaches, expect to pay big dollar resort prices. If a 5 mile drive is acceptable, prices get a lot more reasonable.

Keep in mind that the east and north sides of each island are generally rainier and wetter than the west and south sides, so property on the west and south costs more. Also, bear in mind that elevation (a corollary to distance from the beach) has an effect on temperature; close to the beach will be warmer than inland and up-country. Although the weather is always near-perfect everywhere, your idea of perfect might be a little warmer or colder than mine. As an example, Waikoloa Village, at an elevation of about 900 ft and about 6 miles from the coast, is about 7 to 10 degrees cooler than Waikoloa Beach. Waimea, yet another 1000-or-so feet higher, is cool enough that people sometimes wear coats and shoes and things.

Picking a place to live in Hawai'i, whether it be renting or buying, can have complications. Some things are obvious, and probably applicable anywhere, while others are unique to Hawai'i.

- Don't buy or rent without seeing it first. Seems obvious, but….

- Have your financing lined up ahead of time. Chances are good that your bank doesn't do business in Hawai'i.

- Don't put yourself mentally in a home before you're actually in the home; it's a setup for disappointment.

- Have a good working relationship with a real estate agent you trust.

- Houses can cost a lot. Housing prices are about on a par with the California coast, and you will have to have hurricane insurance.

- Almost everything is imported, including fuel. Consequently, electricity[35] costs about 3 times what you're used to, and there are virtually no gas appliances.

---

35 Hawai'i is also one of those places where solar stuff makes economic sense. Solar water heaters cut the electricity bill by about a third, and photovoltaic electric generation is sensible and profitable. Solar installations in Hawai'i have as of this writing about a 3 year break-even period, after which the cost is zero and the electric bill drops to the basic connection charge of ~$20.

- Since the climate is pretty much perfect, there's also usually no heat, and in many places, no air conditioning. People in Hawai'i live close to the environment; if it's too warm, they open a window. If it's too cool, they close the window.

- Houses are generally smaller than most places in the US. People in Hawai'i spend a lot of time outdoors, which is pretty much the best reason for living there.

- Some common municipal utilities are different; in many areas, waste is handled by cesspool or septic tank, trash is hauled by the homeowner to a transfer station, etc.

- Potable water can be scarce in some drier areas.

- Something you'll see a lot; people take of their shoes before entering. Usually no big deal since you're wearing flip-flops[36], right?

Homes everywhere reflect their environment and their inhabitants. Homes in Hawai'i are open and friendly, like the people.

---

36   We call them "slippers", actually.

Hawaiian Transportation

Not surprisingly, the Hawaiian Islands are pretty sparsely populated, making getting around more of a challenge than, say, New York City; or in some ways, Montana. With the exception of the metropolitan Honolulu area, there isn't really any local public transportation[37], and inter-island transportation is by air unless you're an unusually hardy, Polynesian Islander-type with an outrigger canoe and a lot of confidence. If you were such a person, you wouldn't be reading this. So, you can fly from island to island (at this time, no ferries, either, except Maui to Lanai; the only regular sea-going

---

37   Hawai'i Island does have a bus service that goes around the island on a virtually incomprehensible schedule.

human transportation is the occasional cruise ship), and drive, slowly, from place to place on the island. We all know how to manage the airplane end of things, so let's talk about the driving.

Distances in Hawai'i tend to be long (surprisingly); population centers are around the periphery of each island, generally at locations originally influenced by the availability of good ocean access. Roads generally follow the coast line because that's where the population is, and it's easier to build the road on a more-or-less constant grade along the coast than go up and over a mountain.

Hawai'i roads can be steep; the islands are the tips of undersea mountains, and the slopes are pretty fierce, even paralleling the coast, partly because of the way the roads are laid out. Roads are narrow, twisty, and generally slow by nature. With the exception of the Interstate[38] highways on O'ahu, island speed limits are generally 55 mph, and sometimes that's generous. This is probably a good idea, since there is also a certain amount of wildlife that occasionally feels the need to share the road with you; wild goats, pigs, donkeys, chickens, and turkeys, to name a few.

Since most roads are two lane and often look like they were laid out by a drunken goat, traffic moves at the pace of the slowest vehicle, which can be pretty slow. You just can't make good time, and that's how it goes. The roads are pretty basic in nature, being a strip of asphalt poured on the ground, with a stripe up the middle, and not a lot of roadway preparation; no elaborate cut

---

38   One might ask, "Interstate"? Yes, it's true.

and fill operations, just asphalt laid on the ground. On the good side of things, since there are no freeze-thaw conditions and few big trucks, the surfaces are generally in good shape, with few potholes. The biggest problem with Hawai'i roads is that, despite the relatively low population, there is just too much traffic.

Also on the good side of the ledger, there are few big trucks. Those of us who have traveled on a busy interstate, and by that I mean everyone, know the Peterbilt population can be intimidating. Not so in Hawai'i; there are a few cement trucks, a few gas tankers, and the occasional semi hauling a freight container. Otherwise, the truck population is limited to local delivery trucks[39]. Think about it; there is no need to haul bulk freight from one place to another far away, since there is no place far away that can be reached by truck easier than by water. Thus, no long-haul trucks, no incomprehensible CB chatter, no dead alligator-looking tire treads in the road. It makes Hawai'i roads less intimidating.

Another thing to keep in mind is that gas is expensive; about the same, or a little more or less, than gas in Los Angeles, depending on where you are. The combination of long distances and expensive gas would seem like it would keep traffic down, but that doesn't appear to be the case. However, hitchhiking is a viable means of transportation here.

So, how do you get around? If you're visiting, or just arrived, you have one choice in transportation; rent a

---

39   A big exception, on the Big Island, at least, is military traffic going to/from training areas and ports. Armored big-stuff is intimidating. Fortunately, it's also slow-moving, but tanks, etc ALWAYS have the right-of-way, even if they don't.

car[40]. All of the airports have substantial rental operations, and the rates are semi-reasonable. A good half of
the cars are convertibles (excellent choice), and everything from econoboxes to land yachts with their own
ZIP codes can be had. The government of the State of
Hawai'i recognizes this rental car business as a terrific
source of revenue that doesn't adversely affect the resident population and slaps on some horrific taxes, but
even so, the rates are decent, probably because there is
a lot of competition and the cars are utilized continuously, no slow season or down time. It is not unusual
to get a current-model-year rental car with 30,000 miles
on the odometer and the seat still warm from the last
occupant. Rental cars get used. A lot.

By the time a rental car is retired, it's had more wet
bottoms on the seats than a case of diapers, and collected enough sand to make a decent beach. I'm trying to
say that the car will show some cosmetic signs of use[41].
There may be a fine collection of small dings, dents,
chips, and scratches, and a wear item unique to Hawai'i,
salt stains on the seat belts. Mechanically, though, the
rentals get serviced and anything likely to wear or break
(such as brakes; Hawai'i is hard on car brakes because
it's lots and lots of steep hills) gets fixed; a tourist sitting
by the road in his broken-down rental is a tourist not
likely to rent from that company again (not to mention
lost revenue during the breakdown).

40 Old Hawaiian joke; what's the difference between a 4 wheel drive and a
    rental car? Rental cars can go anywhere.

41 In a tribute to modern car upholstery, it actually survives much better
    than, say, the average theatre carpet. That stuff they upholster car seats
    with is tough.

A notable exception to the high-wear phenomenon is Enterprise, which would apparently prefer that you not actually use the car, just look at it. They will charge you, a lot, for sand, dirt, pet hair, smoke, and probably bad vibes. Their cars do look pretty good, though.

When the rental cars have served their tour of duty they get sold. Some are sold on the islands, of course; but there is a surfeit, so the rest are shipped to the mainland and appear on used car lots in Albuquerque[42] and elsewhere. If I were shopping for a used rental, I'd look at Enterprise because they really, really don't like to rent their cars, but unfortunately, their prices reflect that.

People who live here have more choices in transportation.

A lot of locals do buy these used rentals; and why not? They're already here, they've had at least the minimum required service and maintenance, and the prices aren't too awful.

There are new car dealerships as well, and the prices reflect the cost of shipping the car from the mainland and the general scarcity of competition, which can add thousands of dollars to the price. Plus, being new car dealers, they have an apparent mandate to ask ridiculous prices[43]. Still, this is an option.

Craigslist and, of course, the classified ads are a resource that should be familiar to mainlanders, and so should the caveats that apply to both. Craigslist ads in

---

42 We bought one of these on the mainland, a pretty nice, late model convertible with salt-stained seatbelts and well-used brakes, and 30,000 miles. Good car, too.

43 Some uncharitable people say that car dealers in Hawai'i should be buried with a stake through their hearts.

particular can be fraught with convenient omissions of fact, and just plain misrepresentations. We won't discuss the often hilarious Craigslist ads here; that's a worthy subject all on its own. Just know that, surprisingly, the cashier's check from that Nigerian prince won't clear your bank, legitimate sellers don't sell current-year BMW's for $1500, and there is no free lunch.

New immigrants have another choice; they can ship their own car from the mainland, an interesting process[44]. It takes about 3 weeks plus a couple of months of advance notice to ship a car, and costs a about $1100 as of 2013. The cars are either loaded on big ships designed for odd and oversized cargo, sharing space with military freight and heavy machinery, or put into containers[45], and off-loaded at the major harbors on each island. The same ships will transport cars between islands, so it's possible to buy a car on O'ahu and ship it to Maui relatively easily. Aside from the necessity of dropping off a car at one port and picking it up 3 weeks later at another, this is a pretty painless process. If this is too hard to manage (and it can require the services of a cooperative brother-in-law), the shipping company will arrange for take your car to the departure port, at the usual rates for car transport.

If you bring in a car from the mainland this way, you will need some paperwork and some patience, but the process is actually pretty simple. You need to make

44 Actually, in some cases, it might be attractive for residents to buy a car on the mainland and ship, despite shipping costs and Hawai'i taxes on imported new cars.

45 If it's a big enough container, you can ship your car and household goods all at once, yet another option.

reservations with the shipping company well in advance, for one thing. The car needs to be clean[46], and empty of pretty much everything; you can't smuggle in extra baggage in your trunk (unless, of course, you have your own container for car and household goods. The procedures are different for shipping a car and shipping a car as part of a containerized shipment).

Once landed (cars are delivered to a major port on each island), you have 30 days to re-register in Hawai'i. The process is pretty simple and painless, especially if you are used to mainland motor vehicle departments. You get your first annual safety inspection at one of the many places licensed to do so (some of them think you need an appointment for the 10 minute inspection process. Since it's the same $20 or so everywhere, you might as well go to a place that is OK with drop-ins), and take the inspection certificate, the mainland registration and title, your proof of insurance, and $5.50 cash or check—no credit cards or debit cards— (on Hawai'i Island; it varies from island to island, but the most expensive is $10) to a DMV office. They will issue a new title and registration, and two new license plates. You then return to the inspection station with your license plates and registration and get your inspection sticker. Thereafter, you will need an annual inspection at which time they simply peel off the old sticker and install a new one.

Hawai'i honors your existing registration fee; that means that if your current registration expires in

---

46   For agricultural inspection for foreign weed seeds, snakes hidden in the wheel wells, etc. Also so damage, if any, can be seen and documented.

January, so will you Hawai'i registration. You don't pay any additional fees when you register unless the vehicle is new and being imported, in which case there is a tax. You'll get a notice in the mail that the new registration is due, at which time you will pay the full, weight-based Hawai'i registration fee.

In many ways this is probably the best choice if you have a decent car already, considering that cars in Hawai'i can get pretty beat and new cars are priced to gladden the heart of the most avaricious dealer[47].

Chances are, whatever car you have, if it's in good order, will be fine. Just pay the freight, it'll be less than the premium you'll pay for a replacement on the Hawai'i end.

The climate is generally excellent all the time, so a lot of locals get around by motorcycle or scooter. It is not uncommon to see a tiny 49cc motor scooter[48] with a boogie board sideways in front of the driver buzzing down the highway at a stately pace, with a 2-mile-long train of cars behind it. Where possible, the scooter pilots will use the shoulder, as do bicyclists, who abound, but sometimes, there just isn't one.

Scooters and motorcycles have the advantages of super fuel economy and easy parking; you'd think this wouldn't be an issue, but it is. Again, many of the towns are 18th and 19th century sailing villages, designed for

---

47 Almost every dealer we talked with added really outrageous markups to the MSRP, plus dealer-installed "protection packages" and the like. The "justification" for this is that the market is small so they have to make extra profit.

48 These little tiddlers need a one-time registration, no big annual fees, so they're quite popular. Plus, they deliver about a zillion miles per gallon.

foot traffic. Two wheelers can also be cheap to buy[49]. Some of the scooters retail new for less than $1000 and there's always something on Craigslist that can be had for sofa-cushion change.

One curious fact about persons in Hawai'i is that they generally don't have a lot of self esteem tied up in their vehicle. Cars, trucks, scooters, etc are a means to an end, and that end generally involves getting to the beach, the store, and home. True, there are some pristine luxury cars, some badly-out-of-place super sports cars, and some "I'm tough!" jacked up trucks[50], but a lot of the vehicles are just plain ratty. Rust is a standard decoration, missing pieces are normal, and dents are viewed as badges of honor. Minivans all have racks for surf boards, and probably 75% of the cars have either terrycloth or neoprene wet suit fabric seat covers. These cars get used for fun, not for prestige.

A couple of things about registering cars in Hawai'i. There is, as already mentioned, an annual safety inspection, in which the inspector looks for obvious safety defects such as doors falling off. Of course, all the lights have to work, as do brakes, horn, wipers, etc. and the windshield can't be obscured in front of the driver. All

---

49 But not necessarily cheap to maintain. A great fallacy is that a $30,000 motorcycle that needs $500 worth of tires and $500 worth of service every 3000 miles, but gets 40 mpg, is cheaper to operate than a $15,000 car that needs tires every 50,000 miles and $50 worth of service every 5000 miles, but only gets 25 mpg. Many persons, mostly female, will themselves to believe this because their husband said so when he bought the new Harley.

50 Generally without that common denominator of trashiness, plastic testicles hanging from the trailer hitch; something we are all, but especially parents of young children, grateful for.

cars (and motorcycles and scooters) have a safety inspection sticker on the rear; failing to have a current sticker results in a hefty fine. The requirements are minimal, but they're dead serious. You need both the inspection and proof of insurance to drive a car in Hawai'i.

Speaking of insurance, Hawai'i is a no-fault state for liability, which means that you can't be easily sued. Your company covers you, the other guy's company covers him. It's also one of the states where liability insurance is "stacked"; your total liability coverage is the sum of your individual coverages. Owners of multiple cars benefit from this because the individual coverage limits can be lower and still yield the same coverage. A lot of mainland companies don't write policies in Hawai'i, so check this out. Naturally, insurance is probably more expensive than you're used to (a common theme).

Annual registration fees are based on the weight of the vehicle. This means that the older, bigger, heavier, road-crushing land yacht pays a heftier annual fee than the little efficient econobox. The fees vary slightly from island to island, but as an example, a 3500 lb vehicle pays about $150/year on Hawai'i Island. And by the way, the license plates (both of them) stay with the car throughout its life.

Initial registration is expensive for new cars. If a car is registered in Hawai'i within a year of the date on which it was first registered elsewhere, the buyer pays an additional tax of 3% of the value on top of everything else. To put this another way, new cars, and used cars brought from the mainland that are less than one year old, get stuck with a hefty tax; thus, new-ish used cars are cherished perhaps more than they would otherwise be. This does seem like something intended to "help" island car dealers, doesn't it? There is some good news; there is no tax levied on private vehicle sales, and title transfer costs $5.

A Hawai'i driver's license opens the door to local, or *kama'aina,* discounts. You will need some proof of legal residency, including a social security card and original birth certificate or passport, to get one. Hawai'i has some driving laws that differ a bit from other states, but then again, what state doesn't have its own unique laws? Best bet is to download the on-line license manual, study the 150 questions, and take the test. The 30 questions on the test will be taken from the manual verbatim.

The weather is nearly perfect; have we said that? Consequently, there are a lot of bicycle riders, despite the sometimes-difficult distances and terrain. It is not unusual to see a chain of bicycle riders dressed like color blind superheros strung out along the shoulder of the road 20 miles from the nearest anything[51]. Certainly, this is a transportation option for the very fit, but probably not something for most of us. Those hills are steep.

Another viable option, at least on the Big Island, is hitchhiking. It's very common and reliable; so much so that I know people who hitchhike to their regular jobs. It's not unusual to see kids hitchhiking to visit their friends in another town or hitching a ride to the beach, surfboard and all. You might not want to do this if you have a plane to catch. Or you might; I've seen hitchhikers looking for a ride to the airport, complete with backpacks, etc.

---

51   Especially as the annual Ironman triathlon approaches.

Honolulu and environs are a special case. Honolulu is a bustling city, with a functional bus system, the beginnings of a light rail system, and traffic jams. While Kailua Kona, for example, has slow traffic around the airport about half an hour after one of the dozen or so daily trans-oceanic flights lands and 300 tourists head out to their resorts, Honolulu has a more conventional, 8 am and 5 pm, rush hour. Watching the news on TV (mostly broadcast out of Honolulu) from a neighbor island, one gets the impression that there's a whole separate world of traffic out there. And there is.

Transportation in Hawai'i is in some ways simpler than on the mainland; you never need to worry about the weather, no one will think less of you if you drive a rustbucket, and the question of taking the bus or train vs. driving is rarely an issue.

Weather in Hawai'i

Hawai'i weather forecasts are easy, but the TV weather guys and gals try to make it more dramatic than it is[52].

Weather at a given location in Hawai'i is pretty consistent. Temperatures don't change much from day to night and season to season, winds are pretty much the same, and it's nicely predictable. Even the rainfall is consistent. If you have general climatic data about a location[53] you pretty much have the current and forecast

---

52 Notable exceptions to boring weather; hurricane, tsunami, eruption of the volcano you happen to be living on. With the exception of a hurricane, these are not really weather-related, but they sure take care of the boredom.

53 http://www.rssweather.com/climate/ is a good starting point.

weather. Statistical variations from the norm are small; this means that if the climatic data indicates a daytime high of 82, you can reasonably expect today, tomorrow, and 3 months from Thursday to have a daytime high of 82, give or take a few degrees, unless there's something going on.

Note the key words, "given location". Go a little ways, and you're in an entirely different climactic area. Hawai'i has something for everyone, including some things no one wants. You can find essentially all of the terrestrial climate types, and a few non-terrestrial ones. Desert, arctic tundra, tropical savannah, etc; they're all here. In fact, the currently-erupting volcano, Kilauea, is like nothing else on the surface of the earth. It's more of a surface-of-Mercury sort of thing.

So, you might ask, how does the weather in Hawai'i work? Warning; lecture ahead.

As you've no doubt noticed, Hawai'i is a collection of islands located roughly in the middle of the Pacific Ocean, about 2500 miles as the 757 flies from California. The islands are small, relative to continents at least, and the ocean is big. This lends a certain scientific purity to the Hawaiian weather; it's oceanic weather, modified only by the fact that the islands stick up a bit. A very big bit, but still small compared to the scope of the ocean.

Hawai'i happens to be located slightly north of the equator, so the prevailing wind is a steady breeze from the northeast (the trade winds, so called because in the days of sailing ships the breeze brought trading ships directly to the islands). When these moist, warm winds encounter mountains, they are forced to rise, cooling in the process. As this air cools, the moisture condenses just like water on the outside of a cold glass, and it rains. Each of the islands has one or more pretty good sized mountains in the middle, so those winds from the northeast are forced to rise when they encounter the island. Consequently, the northeast coasts of the islands have lots and lots of rain; the bigger the mountain, the more rain. The big island, confusingly named Hawai'i, has the biggest mountains, and has a lot of rain on the northeast.

The part of each island southwest of the mountains, however, gets relatively little rain because the air coming down the mountain is relatively dry, because the water rained out on the other side, and the air warms as it descends and compresses. This "rain shadow" effect means that the south and west sides of each island are drier and warmer than the northeast.

Because the islands are small compared to the Pacific Ocean or to a continent, the islands themselves have little effect on the weather[54] other than the "over the mountain" effect of creating rain. The land masses simply aren't big enough to affect air temperature significantly. The temperature of the air when it encounters land at the northeast corner of the island is the temperature of the air over the ocean in that vicinity, which doesn't vary much because the Pacific Ocean is really big.

---

54 Although the big mountains of Mauna Loa, Mauna Kea, and Haleakela, sticking up about 3 miles, may act to divert some weather events from the east away from Hawai'i and Maui. These mountains stick up so far that they form a partial windbreak, forcing storms to flow to the north and south of the mountains.

So, the short version is that the overall sea-level temperature is pretty close to the temperature over the Pacific Ocean in that vicinity, which doesn't vary much. Temperature at a given location is pretty much the over-water temperature, modified by elevation and asphalt cover. Rainfall is similarly predictable, being largely dependent on where on the island you are[55].

"But what about tomorrow's weather?", you might ask. "Is it always 82 degrees and sunny?" Well, sometimes that air coming from the northeast might be a little cooler, or have a little more, or less, moisture, and that will affect how much rain falls, and how warm or cool it's going to be. Pretty much, though, tomorrow is going to be somewhat like today, unless there's something else, like a big storm going on, in which case you can bring up the satellite and radar data on your home computer, or just watch the TV weather guy. He generally has it nailed.

A Few Words About Words—The Hawaiian Language

The Hawaiian language is very unlike English; to the visitor, it may seem that every word begins with "k", followed by strange gargling sounds. Written Hawaiian, first codified by Christian missionaries in the early 19th century, is not any easier; many of the combinations are just not found in English. To compound matters, place names, street names, even everyday words we use all the time are in Hawaiian.

Some of the difficulty comes from the fact that there are no fricatives ("f" sound) or sibilants ("s" sound) in Hawaiian. My wife, being from El Paso, is a fluent Spanish speaker, and is used to its soft sounds and melodious accents. Hawaiian, with its hard stops and consonants, is, well, very foreign to her.

If you want to seem less like an outsider, you'll need to be able to pronounce some Hawaiian words correctly. So, with full credit to Albert J. Schutz's excellent little book "*A Pocket Guide to the Hawaiian Language*", and various on-line resources, here're some basics.

Every letter is pronounced. Fortunately, there are only 12 of them; the 5 vowels we all know, and 7 consonants. The vowels are, for the most part, pronounced like short vowels in English (except "o", which is a long "o"). There are long and short vowels in Hawaiian; the difference is subtle. A long vowel last longer than a short one; that's why it's a long vowel. Easy. It does change the word meaning, though.

The consonants have pretty much the English pronunciation, with a few twists. "W" is sometimes a "v", and sometimes a "w" with a hint of "v". There's no fixed rule, you just have to hear it.

There are also eleven diphthongs, but they should be familiar to an English speaker as well.

Now it gets to be more fun; there are also two special punctuation marks;

- The Kahakō, which is a little line over the letter, indicating that it's a long vowel, and
- The Okina, which is a backwards apostrophe ´ and indicates a glottal stop between syllables; sort of like the English "uh, oh!" Think of it as another consonant.

Unfortunately, street signs and the like don't always include these special symbols, which can leave you guessing about pronunciation.

But wait! There's more!

All syllables end in a vowel. Always. They might start with a vowel, or be just a single vowel (some Hawaiian words are entirely composed of vowels), but there's always a vowel at the end of a syllable. This may well be the single most important rule of Hawaiian pronunciation. If you see a vowel followed by a consonant, you are looking at a syllable break. If you see two vowels together, it's either a diphthong, or a syllable break between the vowels. If the two vowels are identical it is definitely a syllable break. An okina is a consonant and is always a syllable break. For shorter words, an accent is almost always on the second to last vowel, on any long vowel, or on the first letter of a diphthong. Words can have more than one syllable accented. Longer words are often made up of shorter words strung together, so there can be a lot of accented syllables. And, of course, there are always exceptions. In general, follow these simple rules and while you might miss the accent from time to time, you'll probably get the general pronunciation right.

Here are a few common words; the emphasized syllable is italicized.

Aloha — Ah-low-*ha* — Hello, good by, general purpose well wishing, spirit of good will.

Mahalo — Ma-*hah*-low —Thank you, you're a great person.

Mahalo Nui — Ma-*hah*-low *New*-ee — Big thank you.

Makai — Ma-(*k*)*eye* — towards the ocean.

Mauka — *Mow* (like wow)-ka — inland, towards the mountain.

Easy, right? Well, maybe not; but you'll get the hang of it. When you come across a complicated word, just parse it out, and remember that every syllable ends in a vowel. Here're a few tricky ones.

Pu'ukohola   Pu 'u ko ho la
Kamehameha   Ka me ha me ha
Opukaha'ia   O pu ka ha 'i a
Anaeho'omalu   A nae ho 'o ma lu

Hawaiian Politics

Hawai'i is Democratic; not just a little, or by a slim margin, but to the point where one can assume that whoever one is talking with is a Democrat. Fortunately, no one gets especially worked up about it.

This is good news if you're fed up with campaign advertising. It is not a swing state. Presidential candidates don't even bother visiting us, it's a foregone conclusion how our 4 electoral votes will go. We're spared a lot of the invective, leaving room for local candidates' campaigns, which tend to be much more polite.

Not that Hawai'i hasn't experimented. Linda Lingle, a Republican, was governor from 2002 to 2010, making her the second Hawai'i Republican governor, ever. Then again, Ms. Lingle isn't your average anything, either[56]. Still, the state is overwhelming Democratic, with only 1 of the 25 state senators of the Republican persuasion, and 7, out of 51, Republican representatives.

Why? One might ask. I believe there are two main reasons; one rooted in the basic nature of Hawaiians, and the other, historical.

One underlying reason for the Hawaiian preference for Democratic politics is based in the Hawai'i psyche, in the concept of *ohana*; family and interconnectedness. This is not just limited to Native Hawaiians; persons who's family originated from Japan, China, and Korea share the same strong family-like ties. Even us late-coming *haole*[57] feel this. We're on an island in the middle of a big ocean; all-together-in-the-lifeboat feelings are inescapable.

When we watch the weather report on TV, we see a giant globe behind the talking head weatherman, with our islands in the middle of a really big blue area of nothing-ness. The fringes of North and South America are way over on the right edge, and the fringes of Japan and China are way over on the left edge, Australia is somewhere down at the bottom, and we're all alone in the middle. We have to stick up for one another because our homeland, wherever it might be, is very far away. In many ways we act like one big tribe, and are naturally drawn to the political party that is more likely to favor social welfare and support programs.

56　For one thing, she was the only Jewish Republican governor in the US. She's also female, single, likes cats, wears incredibly unflattering glasses, and has a very soft, soothing voice.

57　Caucasians; a not-entirely-flattering term, depending on how it's used.

This is a much more real phenomenon than, say, being from Iowa or being Oakland Raiders fans. Those are what the late Kurt Vonnegut called a *"false karass*[58]*"*; a group of people who imagine that they have a connection that does not really exist. In Hawai'i, we really are alone, and believe that our destinies really are connected. We must care for one another, and therefore are more likely to support the political party that espouses social programs.

Another, very important reason has to do with something I've touched on briefly; Hawai'i's former status as an independent country that was subjugated by force and deceit, and absorbed into the United States as a subject territory.

Hawai'i had very little contact with the rest of the world until the early 19th century, with the arrival of sailors and missionaries. These were soon followed by businessmen and adventurers eager to exploit this new and prosperous place. Soon, Hawai'i was a major exporter of food (including, ironically, oranges to California) and a center of trade. Soon also, much of the new industry, primarily massive sugar plantations, was owned by a few wealthy corporations. These corporations, generally known as the "Big Five", wielded considerable power in Hawai'i since they effectively owned all of the industry and controlled most of the land. In fact, they had so much power that on January 14, 1893, the "Committee of Public Safety", organized and supported by the Big

---

58 If, by some strange quirk of fate, this should become required (or even optional) reading in a middle school somewhere, here's an assignment; read *Cat's Cradle* and write a report on *karass* and *false karass*. This will appeal to the middle-schooler because it's a chance to say "ass".

Five, overthrew Queen Lili'uokalani and openly seized power. United States Marines and sailors intervened in support, effectively sanctioning the overthrow. At that point, Hawai'i in effect became the property of those five large corporations.

The Queen urged her subjects to not resist with violence and to avoid bloodshed, confident that the United States' treaty obligations to Hawai'i would be honored. Instead, the United States government, led by President Benjamin Harrison, recognized the "Republic of Hawai'i", thus abdicating its treaty obligations to the monarchy.

Hawai'i remained a nominal republic for about 5 years until annexed to the United States as a territory in 1898. The Big Five companies remained in control for the next 50 years, through a Republican-dominated legislature firmly controlled by the Big Five.

Beginning in the 1930's, in response to decades of ill treatment, poor wages, and general abuse, residents of Hawai'i staged a series of strikes, boycotts, and civil disobedience that culminated in the so-called "Hawai'i Democratic Revolution" of 1954, in which essentially all of the Republican members of the legislature were voted out of office and replaced by members of the Hawai'i Democratic Party. While this did not end the power of the Big Five, it restored considerable influence to the majority of the residents. In 1959 Hawai'i became a state, further weakening the almost feudal power of the Big Five.

This happened not so long ago. Native Hawaiians and long-time residents continue to resent the historic role of the United States in general and the Republican party in particular for their roles in overthrowing the legitimate government and pressing most of the population into virtual serf-dom. In 2003 the Congress of the United States apologized to the Native Hawaiians for the US' role in the overthrow of the monarchy in 1893. At the same time, the United Church of Christ also offered a public apology for that denomination's complicity in the overthrow. Both apologies acknowledged that the overthrow of the monarchy was an illegal act in the light of international law.

Hawaiian self-government and recognition of Native Hawaiians as a political and ethnic entity is a recurring them in Hawaiian politics, with excursions into Hawaiian sovereignty. The "Akaka Bill", named for its sponsor, former Senator Daniel Akaka, sought recognition of Native Hawaiians as a separate entity. Be aware that this is a sensitive issue.

Walk Like a Hawaiian—Quick Summary of Life in Hawai'i

What's it like to be a full-time resident of Hawaii, you might ask? Pretty nice. Here're some semi-random tidbits.

Who is a Hawaiian?

This may be confusing; in every other state, the residents are either *"Xxxx-ans"* or some cute term like *"Sooners"* or the like. Not so in Hawai'i. The term "Hawaiian" is reserved for actual, native Hawaiian people, who make up about 20% of the population, and who, understandably, can be a little testy about misuse of their identity[59]. White folks (*haole*, a not altogether flattering term in the local glossary) make up about 25%, Asians of various origins are about 40% of the population, and the rest is a mix. If you are non-native and a resident of Hawai'i, you are still not Hawaiian; about the only general term that might apply is *kama'aina*, a Hawaiian word meaning "child of the land". This is a good thing. If you are visiting, you are a tourist; also a good thing.

Is it Expensive?

Yes. Most things cost more. Gas is particularly expensive, and electricity is right up there too. On the other hand, locals often get discounts from local businesses, which helps. Another factor mitigating the seemingly high prices is that you really don't need, or want, some things. Bye, bye heat bill. Wave goodbye to heavy clothing. Forget those Brooks Brothers' suits. Smaller houses, more time outside doing outdoors things, not worrying about what the neighbors think of the 15-year-old car sitting in the driveway, all keep actual expenses under control. After all, almost two million people seem to make it work.

What Do People in Hawaii Do for Work?

Everything, but a lot of it has to do with tourism. Hawaii is an island, thoroughly isolated from the rest of the world, including the rest of the United States to

---

59 Think of it in the same manner as identifying yourself by the name of a Native American tribe that happens to live where you do. People from Indiana don't call themselves "Indians", do they?

which it is a latecomer. This island-awareness permeates every aspect of culture. Everybody does something; everybody contributes in some fashion. Even us tired old retired guys take part-time jobs renting cars, mopping up at the local school, giving tours to visitors, or writing books. For one thing, the money is helpful, but more than that, we are all driven by some kind of cultural need to contribute.

Heavy industry is limited; there are small power plants, cement bulk terminals, deep-water ports, heavy equipment maintenance, stuff like that, but no big steel mills or coal mines or the like. Much of the economy is tied to tourism.

We have friends who tele-commute, with occasional visits to the mainland for face-to-face meetings. Financial services, some marketing, graphic and advertising services, writing; anything that can be done by telecommuting on the mainland can be done here.

This might be obvious, but if you are considering moving here with a plan to land a high-paying job after moving, you might re-evaluate your situation. Many employers won't consider applicants who have lived here for a short time because they have a high likelihood of leaving again. And, of course, there aren't a lot of high-paying jobs available, since there isn't much in the way of industry to generate them. While it's possible to live comfortably with a modest income, it's harder than, say, the mainland Midwest. We know people who do OK with their income from selling jewelry in gift shops and fixing roofs, but they don't have a lot left over. We also know people who sell real estate, time shares, and the like, and do very well, but they worked hard to learn the skills and get the local licensing and specialized knowledge. So, it's possible.

If you have work that will let you re-locate and tele-commute, such as graphic arts or investments; or if you have a high-demand specialty, including some construction specialties (roofers, electricians, plumbers, and carpenters are always in demand wherever and whenever there is construction going on), teaching, or nursing; or if you are retired or semi-retired and are confident that your income is adequate, then it should work out fine. If your "plan" is to luck into something while you bus tables, it might not.

What Do You Wear?

First, do **NOT** base your ideas of dress and deportment on *Dog, the Bounty Hunter*[60]. He can get away with it, the rest of us can't. If your vision of how we dress is an aloha shirt, shorts, and flip-flops, you're pretty much spot on; that's for nice occasions. For formal occasions, serious business presentations, etc. we might wear longer pants (I have a pair of white linen pants reserved for such events—the *Emile DeBeque* look is always trendy) and for informal stepping out, a t-shirt is *de rigour*. Women wear pretty much the same thing, or a loose wrap or muu-muu, or old coffee sacks, or whatever was on sale at Walmart, as far as I can tell. Honestly, I really don't know for sure what women wear; it's all over the place. Many women do wear a small fortune in gold

---

60 Unless of course, you are Dwayne Chapman, in which case, keep doing what you're doing.

bracelets, a native Hawaiian tradition, lending a delightful jingle to their walking about. We just don't get too serious about our clothes. Which, come to think of it, is a pretty good summary of clothing, and other things, in Hawai'i. There's an indefinable casualness (or as some more tightly wound mainlanders might say, slovenliness) about how we dress; difficult to say exactly what it is, but one can generally tell the locals from the visitors at a glance.

That's when we're not in the water; for swimming, diving, surfing, etc we wear pretty much what everyone else does, bathing suits[61]. Serious divers, surfers, etc might wear a wetsuit if they plan to be in the water for a while, since even warm water saps the body's heat.

You won't need shoes often, but hiking boots can be useful. You will probably not need that down jacket in your closet. Never, unless you plan to visit the top of Mauna Kea. Give it to charity now, or ask your family in Alaska to store it for when you come to visit.

What do you Eat?

Pretty much what you eat. Probably less beef, since it's expensive (although premium grass fed beef is raised on the Big Island and can be had at a reasonable price), more fish, which can be less expensive, and there are varieties that never make it to mainland supermarkets. I recommend Walu and Ono as two good choices; I will eat Ono anything. (As an aside, the Hawaiian word *"ono"* also means "delicious"; appropriate, in this case),

---

61   There are, of course, exceptions. While public nudity is not legal, there are a few isolated informally nude beaches.

pork (Kalua pork and cabbage is a popular Hawaiian delicacy), vegetables (again, often local, and the best), fruit. Tropical fruit is generally super cheap, things like apples are imported and cost a bundle. There are some exquisite banana varieties that Chiquita doesn't sell. If you like Asian food, food in Hawai'i will thrill you, as just about everything has some Asian component in its origin. If, on the other hand, big slabs of roast beef and potatoes is your choice, you might not be as happy.

One menu item unique to Hawai'i is the plate lunch; two scoops of rice, a scoop of macaroni salad, and an entre such as chicken katsu or loco moco (a hamburger patty, rice, with an egg on top, covered with brown gravy. Delicious). While this makes dieticians recoil, it doesn't seem to hurt life expectancy any. Or maybe it does; we might live to 100 if we didn't eat plate lunches[62].

Curiously, Spam is a big seller in Hawai'i; people in Hawai'i eat more Spam than anyplace else in the world. Grocery stores sell some interesting, and unique, varieties of Spam. It is even integrated into Oriental food; Spam musubi[63] is a common offering. While I don't particularly care for Spam musubi, one of my dogs loves it. On the other hand, Spam and eggs is hard to beat in the morning.

Speaking of sushi, you can get spectacularly good, and spectacularly bad. I like a little sushi stand in a shopping center parking lot where the lady rolls up sushi on demand, $6 for a really good spicy tuna roll. At

---

62 Interesting fact; according to the 2010 Census, residents of Hawai'i have the longest life expectancy of any state, 78.21 years.

63 Spam and sticky rice rolled in nori (dried seaweed).

the other extreme is the tourist-oriented fancy sushi place where everything is breaded in panko and deep fried, with names like "Torched Kona Kampichi--$27".

There are some world-class restaurants as well. *Merriman's, Roy's, Alan Wong's*[64], are all local, first-class restaurants worth seeking out if you're in the mood to spend some serious money for serious food. At a slightly lower level, you can find pretty good, small local places. *Zippy's* is *Denny's* with a Hawaiian flavor, *L&L Hawaiian Barbecue* is what it sounds like, *Big Island Grill* is a local favorite in Kona.

Although Hawai'i as a whole is a net importer of food, one local crop stands out; coffee. Kona coffee is arguably[65] among the world's best, as is Ka'u coffee from the south end of the island and Kaua'i-grown coffee. In fact, nearly all Hawaiian coffees are excellent. Like food in Italy, you cannot find a bad cup of coffee in Hawaii. Good Kona can be had for about $20/pound, good Hawaiian blends suitable for everyday guzzling are about $7/pound, and even the priciest, fanciest Kona, each cherry carefully picked by beautiful virgins and roasted during the new moon over a fire of dollar bills while the roasters chant and sacrifice a goat, are still two-digit prices. You never have to drink Folger's again. If you like coffee, come to Hawai'i. If you don't like coffee, come anyway; maybe you've never had good coffee.

---

64   Alan Wong's is in Honolulu. Worth the trip.

65   Only arguable among people who don't really like coffee. The rest of us are convinced. We use those other coffees for kitty litter.

What do People do for Fun?

Ha. What don't we do? Naturally, anything associated with water sports is in[66], including things not found elsewhere; not too many other places where recreational outrigger canoeing is popular, or kite surfing, or things like that. Snorkeling and diving are naturals; the water is clear as glass in most places, and the underwater population is spectacular.

Some folks like to get a little closer to that underwater population. Deep sea fishing for fish not found in, say, the Colorado River, is readily available, but be warned that any fish you catch belong to the boat, not to you, unless you've made prior arrangements.

For some reason, every resort and town with a population over about 20 has a golf course; I guess for the non-water-sports people. Some of the courses are designed by famous golf people such as Robert Trent Jones. Greens fees range from $8 for a municipal course in Hilo (and I believe there's both a senior and *kama'aina* discount available on top of that) to over $350 at some of the resorts.

Hiking is popular, all of the islands are seriously mountainous and for the most part gifted with spectacular vegetation, wildlife, and views; taking photographs of these same spectacular views are equally popular. I believe you would have to work at it to take a really bad landscape photo here.

---

66 Hawai'i is the undisputed drowning capital of the US. Never, ever, turn your back on the ocean. Those waves have a long way to build up energy. Interestingly, though, more than half of all drownings occur in water less than 3 feet deep; they could have saved themselves by standing up.

Hawaii seems to be a magnet for bicycle riders. They can be seen in their colorful costumes[67] and native habitat along the "major" highways (Queen Ka'ahumanu Highway on the Big Island was designed with bicycles in mind) and peddling frantically up and down the volcanos. A popular tourist activity on Maui is a dawn trip to the top of Haleakala to catch the spectacular sunrise, with a bicycle ride back down. It takes about 4 hours for the round trip, and sunrise from the top is stunning. Of course, the dedicated cyclist rides up the volcano, too, all 10,000+ feet of it.

The Big Island is home to the original Iron Man Triathalon (relocated from O'ahu), which consists of a 2.4 mile swim in the ocean, followed by a 112 mile bicycle ride, followed by a 26.2 mile marathon run, done one after another with no breaks or vacations in between. Contestants have 17 hours to do the whole thing. This takes physical endurance to a whole new level; yet it's so popular that there are way more potential contestants than openings[68]. A significant portion of the Big Island population volunteers to support the event.

Not quite unique to Hawai'i is amateur astronomy. The seeing is generally spectacular, and with very little effort can be improved to best-in-the-world status by driving even part-way up Mauna Kea, where superscopes such as the twin 10 meter Keck telescopes and

---

67 Bicyclists, at least serious ones, all dress for safety, I suppose; either to be seen, or to scare people and animals away.

68 The story is that three super-athletes were boasting about each of their sports, claiming that theirs was the most difficult. In a fit of something-or-other, they decided to create a new one combining all of their individual ones. It wears me out to just think about it.

8.3 meter Subaru telescopes, along with nearly two dozen others[69], live. Even in light-polluted urban areas, a spectacular view of the sky can be seen.

What Other Surprises are Waiting?

The above not withstanding, all is not perfect in paradise. There are a few issues not obvious to the casual resort visitor that might be a negative for some. For instance, insects and non-domestic critters are a normal feature of the tropics, and Hawai'i has them in abundance. While there are no snakes in Hawai'i[70], there are roaches of all sizes, flying beetles the size of walnuts (nearly), centipedes that look like pieces of garden hose, and geckos everywhere[71]. Perhaps surprising to some visitors, the islands are 100% volcanic. Depending on the extent of weathering, the soil will range from stain-your-clothes reddish-brown to stark black rock[72].

The more recognizable areas of the animal kingdom are represented by a number of now-feral, but formerly domesticated, creatures such as chickens, turkeys, cats, goats, donkeys, and pigs. The pigs grow to enormous size and are hunted for meat. The goats run to the scrawny end of the size spectrum, have through natural selection assumed the color of the dirt, and browse along the highway. Interestingly, dead animals in the

---

69 http://www.ifa.hawaii.edu/mko/telescope_table.shtml

70 Or, curiously, hummingbirds, which interfere with pineapple pollination.

71 The geckos do eat other insects, and in turn are preyed upon by feral cats.

72 There are two (at least) Hawaiian words for lava; Ah'a is the sharp jagged kind, probably named after what one says walking barefoot on it. Pahoihoi is the smooth flowing kind.

road are a rarity; the feral species also seem to have selected for intelligence[73], at least where it aids survival. The chickens are a noisy nuisance, and are probably too stringy and tough to eat, assuming you could catch one. The turkeys are not as annoying as the chickens, but are bigger and leave messy calling cards, as well as being a novel golf hazard. Donkeys seem to be disappearing, but cats abound. In fact, there are active catch, neuter, and release programs for feral cats.

Perhaps strangely, there is a robust mongoose population. Supposedly, they were imported to prey on rats, but as it happens, mongoose's (or whatever the proper term is) either don't like rat as a diet item, or more likely, hunt at times when rats are not up and about. What they (the mongoose's) do eat are the eggs of the native, and endangered, Hawaiian goose, the Ne'ne. Bad idea.

Some other non-native species such as the voracious Axis Deer were imported for similar "it seemed like a good idea at the time" reasons, now bitterly regretted. Hawai'i Department of Agriculture takes an aggressive stance on animal imports (see chapter on bringing in dogs and cats).

One particularly annoying invasive species is the Coqui Frog, so called because it's very loud cry sounds like "coqui!" It's loud enough to wake one from a sound sleep. This species is found in generally wet areas, and is so annoying that there's a concerted effort to wipe it out. Honolulu County even has an iPhone app for that.

---

73   And it's not that they're shy of humans. They just know to stay out of the roads, probably because those who didn't, aren't; proving Professor Darwin's point.

It is also a dirty place, in the sense of there being a lot of dirt. The wind blows, covering everything with a layer of volcanic soil. Since Hawaiian houses are pretty much open, everything inside gets covered. Dust covers on delicate objects are a must. The fastidious will soon wear themselves out with dusting, and need to go to the beach[74] to recover, where, amazingly, they will discover yet more dirt in the form of sand. If you're a dirt-o-phobe, forget it.

Gardening in Hawaii has a different flavor as well. Mainland gardeners, even those from the most favored locations, are used to nurturing and carefully husbanding their plants. Here, gardening takes the form of killing things. Given a little water, the abundant sunshine and fertile soil will grow just about anything[75], and quickly. No Miracle Gro needed, but lots of Roundup. And a machete.

A caution about gardening. Those tall, majestic palm trees? They can kill. Falling coconuts are a genuine hazard; there's a whole industry around grooming palm trees to remove dead fronds and coconuts. Actually, there's a significant industry focused on gardening and yard care in general, but the coconut hazard is probably not one the newcomer or visitor is likely to expect.

Speaking of plants, there aren't many indoor plants in Hawaii. This may be partly due to the fact that the

---

74 The visitor will note that state park beaches usually have warm fresh water showers. Very nice. By the way, beaches are all state land; no one can legally close a beach, although there are some ways of limiting attendance.

75 Some plants, such as the very attractive Plumeria, or Frangipani, will grow from a stick stuck into the ground.

boundary between indoors and out-of-doors is blurred. It might also be because, well, what would those plants be? The things we treasure as indoor plants during those dark and dreary mainland winters grow wild here.

What about crime? I watch Hawai'i Five-O/Dog the Bounty Hunter etc. and it looks like a lot of crime.

Popular TV shows notwithstanding, Hawai'i is not a notoriously high crime area. Violent crimes are rare (although property crimes such as petty theft are a bit above the national norm). The streets are not filled with high-speed car chases, shootings are very rare, and the Yakuza/Mafia do not control all important businesses. There is, not surprisingly, no special *"Hawai'i Five-O"* crime fighting unit[76]. If you don't believe me, subscribe to the Honolulu Star-Advertiser for a while, or just watch the on-line TV news, where the big excitement is 20 ft waves; here's a starter link—

www.kitv.com

As for Dog, he would be unique anywhere.

No amount of reading about it can truly prepare one for some of these things. Just be a little flexible and it'll all work out.

---

76 Although to be fair, the show is quite popular here. In fact, there is a bronze bust of Jack Lord, the original star of the show back in the '70's, at Kahala Mall.

So What's Not to Like?

There're lots of great things about Hawai'i; how about the not-so-great? There has to be a snake in the garden[77], right? It can't be just kalua pork and frangipani all the time. Are there down-sides?

Well, of course. The potentially not-so-great can be lumped into three broad categories; population, culture, and logistics. Some of this summary is a repeat I've already touched on elsewhere.

First of all, Hawai'i is a small, predominantly rural, state. This can be a huge shock, particularly if you're moving from an urban area. Honolulu, the capital, has

---

77   Not literally. There are no snakes in Hawai'i, and the Department of
      Agriculture works hard to keep it that way.

a population of about 400,000 in the metropolitan area; about the same as New Orleans and Anaheim. Unlike Louisiana and California, the entire state population is only about 1.3 million or so; most of the residents of Hawai'i live in or near Honolulu[78], making it the most densely populated state capital, as a percentage of state population, in the US. In other words, most of the state outside of Honolulu is rural, and Honolulu isn't quite in the same league as Los Angeles. So, a big piece of the culture shock you might (and probably will) experience comes from that demographic.

If you're moving from New York City to Honolulu, it will be different; but then, if you move from The Big Apple to Tucson it will be different too, in a similar way. If you're moving from just about anyplace big enough to be recognizable[79] to anyplace in Hawai'i outside of Honolulu, it's going to be really different. The simple fact of re-locating from an urban area to a very rural one is, all by itself, a shock; and no place in Hawai'i aside from Honolulu can reasonably be called highly urbanized[80].

Hawai'i, including Honolulu, is emphatically not an extension of California. The whole state is small and

---

78   The population of O'ahu, the island on which the city of Honolulu is located, is about 1 million. Confusingly, the island of O'ahu is also the county of Honolulu, which includes the city of Honolulu.

79   That is, a city or town that people outside your county might recognize. If you are moving from, for example, the Four Corners area of the southwest to non-Honolulu Hawai'i, you'll feel instantly at home.

80   Although the metropolitan area has a lot of high-rise buildings, ranking 4th in the nation, behind New York, Chicago, and Los Angeles. This might help urban-relocators feel more at home. http://skyscraperpage. com/cities/?cityID=421&statusID=1

sparsely populated, with services to match. Make no mistake, when you move to Hawai'i, you move to a really rural, thinly-populated place. Pretty much wherever you are moving from, Hawai'i is less densely populated.

Even more important is that this small population is mostly concentrated in one spot. While the cities of Anaheim and Honolulu might have about the same population, Anaheim is cheek-by-jowl with a gazillion other, similar Southern California cities that all sort of blur together to make up the Los Angeles metropolitan area. Honolulu is right up against, well, nothing much. You can't just pop over to the next city to catch a show or shop at Nordstrom's. If it's not in Honolulu, and not at a farmer's market, you likely won't find it locally.

So, unless you're coming from Cedar City, Utah, or someplace equally small and isolated, moving to Hawai'i is moving away from your urban support system. Not that this is a bad thing; but it can be a shock.

We moved from Albuquerque, metropolitan area population nearly 1 million, to Waikoloa, on the Big Island, total island population about 180,000 (Waikoloa counts about 5000 people and half that many cats and dogs). Mainlanders (that's you) think of Albuquerque as a hick town, a figure of fun in Loony Tunes cartoons[81], with an airport so small and quaint that it only has two concourses; a place famous mostly for being the intersection of two Interstate highways, the setting for Breaking Bad, and the neither-confirmed-nor-denied home of a lot of nuclear weapons and people in the federal witness protection program.

---

81   "I knew I should have turned left at Albuquerque"... Bugs Bunny.

The Big Island has one Costco. No Nordstrom's. One and one-half Macy's. No chain "restaurants" like Olive Garden or Applebee's. The nearest theatre to our home in Waikoloa is 24 miles away, and has two screens. The airport in Kailua-Kona, an honest-to-God international terminal, has no jetways, an outdoor passenger waiting area "secured" by a hedge, and passengers walk to the steps leading up to their plane. Residents of Cedar City will feel right at home; everybody else is going to suffer withdrawal symptoms.

Hawai'i is for the most part, rural. Really, really rural (except, of course, Honolulu, which is a big, densely-packed, city).

The rural nature contributes to some of the cultural differences, too. Moving from, say, Los Angeles to Cedar City[82], you're going to not-quite-fit, at least right away. In fact, moving from just about anyplace to anyplace else where you might actually (gasp!) speak with your neighbor, you're going to have an adjustment period. The locals dress differently, talk funny, and generally are "foreign". Or rather, you're foreign. More on this elsewhere.

People in Hawai'i are pretty friendly towards strangers; after all, the economy is based heavily on tourism. We're used to strangers not knowing local customs, driving rules, word pronunciations[83], and their way around. It's not like a life-long New York City-dweller moving to rural Georgia, where nothing fits, and the culture is different in a less-hospitable-to-strangers way.

---

82 Sorry to keep picking on Cedar City; it's a really lovely town.

83 No small thing, considering the Hawaiian language.

Hawai'i has the largest percentage of Asian-American and mixed-ethnicity, and the lowest percentage of Caucasian, residents of any state. *Haole*, or Caucasians, are only about 23% of the population. Needless to say, much of the local culture is heavily influenced by the ethnic diversity[84]. Practically every aspect of daily life, from what's in the grocery store to what we wear, is influenced to some degree by this diversity. If you like Asian food, this is the place for you. If you believe in white supremacy, you will not be wildly popular.

Like any place else, there are people who resent strangers and newcomers, regardless of who or how or why. I was recently treated to a lengthy diatribe about how we *haole* newcomers were displacing the natives, who have to go live in Las Vegas, NV as a result[85] of our thoughtlessness. Strangely, this was from a non-native Caucasian who just happened to move here sooner than I did. I also recently read in the newspaper that a native Hawaiian state legislator was reprimanded by the Speaker of the House for rudeness towards non-natives, including the director of the Department of Land and Natural Resources, proving that racial discrimination works both ways. So far, that's been about the limit of my experience with racial tension. I'm sure it can be there, but I know that we pretty much get what we ask for. I also know that locals have for the most part been quite willing to answer questions, offer help, engage in

---

84 Also needless to say, but I'm saying it anyway, "mixed race" is not an issue. This part is very much not like moving from New York City to rural Georgia.

85 Factoid; Hawaiian Airlines has really good rates to Las Vegas. I'm not sure why this matters, but it apparently does.

conversation, and generally accept me as a fellow human. I think this is a natural outcome of the diversity as well.

That's a really big cultural difference here; there are so many variations on humanity, more than any other state, that lots of us have pretty much given up worrying about it[86].

Many things in Hawai'i are expensive. That's because many things, and nearly all manufactured goods, have to be imported from either the US mainland, Asia, or the South Pacific. Unlike rural areas on the mainland, we can't just bring in lettuce from California by rail or truck, it has to come by sea, a long, slow distance. In fact, that's true of just about everything.

Hawai'i is not food-independent[87]. Much of the land area is unsuited to agriculture, for one thing, although there has been a strong movement towards "food sovereignty" through aquaculture and similar schemes. For another, development in Hawai'i has concentrated more on golf courses than on lettuce farms. So, much of the food is imported. This is slowly changing, but in the long run, we may never see full food independence[88].

Similarly, manufactured goods come from elsewhere, although this is not unique to Hawai'i. We get our iPads and kitchen blenders from giant factories in

---

86 Plus, the generally benevolent living conditions probably help. If you don't need to worry overly much about staying warm or cool or having enough to eat or a place to sleep, life gets a whole lot better.

87 Although it used to be a food exporter, including oranges to California.

88 And this is no different from Los Angeles or Houston or for that matter, Cedar City. The only big difference is the freight cost. And the origin; lettuce from Asia instead of Mexico.

China, the same as the folks in Los Angeles and St. George. The big difference is that they have to come back to us from the mainland, with consequent additional freight costs, because the Hawaiian market simply can't absorb a container ship full of iPads or blenders; back to the population issue again.

I've touched on the small population-limited shopping opportunities; you might be thinking, "I'll just get everything on line!" Good idea, except you're still looking at expensive, and often slow, shipping. UPS to Hawai'i is expensive, FedEx next day air means two days, and parcel post can take an unbelievable length of time[89]. Priority mail is the bright spot in that picture; it takes the same 2 or 3 days it takes anywhere else in the US, and costs the same. "If it fits, it ships" is not an empty motto. Some mainland vendors have figured this out and send smaller packages priority mail, even breaking large shipments into smaller ones to take advantage of the service[90]. Some, unfortunately, are so committed to other services that they simply cannot switch.

This same distance/cost issue might limit your visitors to those who can afford the sometimes-stiff air fare. Grandchildren aren't just going to drop in Sunday afternoon, it's a big exercise in logistics. Depending on how often you want to see the relatives, this can be a good or not-so-good thing.

---

89   I recently had a package that, according to the USPS on-line tracking system, was sitting in Richmond, CA for six weeks. Apparently, the post office waits until they have a ship full, or at least a container full, before sending it.

90   Amazon is a bright spot in this picture. They ship things quickly and inexpensively to Hawai'i.

Hawai'i is rich in potential energy; unfortunately, we don't, or can't, use a lot of it. Hawaiian Electric Company generates a significant portion of electricity from burning of imported fossil fuel, resulting in an electricity cost of about 3 times the national average[91]. On the good side, you won't have much in the way of a heating bill, so if you're moving from a cold climate, rejoice!

Hawai'i as a state has a goal set by the legislature of reducing the carbon footprint to 1990 levels, and to meet 70% of the state energy needs through efficiency and renewable energy generation by 2030. This means more geothermal energy (these are volcanoes, you know), more wind energy, more hydroelectric energy, and more solar energy. Lots and lots of homes in Hawai'i have solar panels on the roof[92] for water heating and electric generation, with more coming. There are substantial state and federal credits for residential solar installations. Taking into account the tax credits and electric bill reductions, installing solar energy stuff yields about a 30% return on investment and a payback period of about 3 years, which is not bad at all.

So most things cost more. You will also find that you might not need as much; as much clothing, as much electricity, as much gasoline, as much eating out or retail therapy.

There are potential downsides to moving to Hawai'i, which may or may not matter to you. If you can let go of

---

91 The spread-out nature of the service area, and the difficult terrain, have an effect here too. Power lines have to cover long distances in some pretty rough areas.

92 Something like 9% of the electric power on Hawai'i Island comes from rooftop solar panels.

instant retail gratification in favor of the many virtues –
climate, friendly people, beaches, then it'll work for you.

We're Not in Kansas Anymore

Hawai'i is really a foreign country where they just happen to accept dollars. There are too many differences, some very subtle, to list them all[93], but the separation from familiar things can weigh especially heavily on the newly-arrived. I read somewhere that a sizeable percentage of people moving here leave in the first few months or years.

If you don't already have friends and/or family in Hawai'i, you might feel a bit isolated. The Hawaiian emphasis on *ohana*, family, is pervasive and powerful.

---

93 Heck, even visiting another state on the mainland can be shocking. Different accents, different food, etc. One indicator of remoteness is that in Hawai'i nothing from the rest of the US is broadcast live because of the time difference..

Weekends and holidays are occasions for family to gather and celebrate something, and there's always something. If you have any affiliations with personal, professional, or any kind of community groups, lean on them for temporary community and start building your *ohana* right away. If you don't have anything like that, or a job, find something. Volunteer for the library or outdoor circle or whale counting (really) or something; anything that will get you out and in contact with people. Having a party is also a really nice start. Having more parties is even better. You're not going to love everybody, but hopefully, you'll find enough fellowship to get things going. After all, your friends and relatives from "back home" are not going to just drop in.

I believe that the emphasis on *ohana* and the isolation and loneliness among the non-attached new arrivals is enhanced by the physical isolation of the islands. On some level, we are all aware of the ocean around us and the distance to any other inhabited land mass. It's not necessarily a conscious thing, but there are very few places in Hawai'i where we are not aware of the ocean.

This is really important. Unless you can create a community, it can be a lonely place.

Getting a job is one way of creating community. The Hawai'i economy is based heavily on tourism, with a dose of military on O'ahu. There isn't an industrial base. If you expect to land a job[94] on arrival, you better do your research and have a skill that fits in. There are three broad classes of jobs;

---

94 Although unemployment in Hawai'i is very low, many of the jobs are equally low.

- Universal skills, doing work that everybody needs. If you're a plumber, a painter, an electrician, a carpenter, a general handyman, an accountant, a mechanic, a teacher, or the like, you can probably find work anywhere, including Hawai'i. Most of these are in short supply and once established, you can reasonably expect to enjoy the standard of living you're used to, but in a nicer climate.

- Rare but needed skills. Top-notch medical, academic, hospitality management, specialty engineering, etc. are examples. If you do something so rare and exotic, but so vital that you can locate at will, you're in. If you're in this category, you already know this and we won't belabor it.

- Hospitality support. Shop clerk, hotel staff (not management; cleaners, valet parking, bell-person), person selling timeshares or snorkel tours, etc. These do not require much in the way of special training, but those who interface with the public do require a high degree of charisma. If you aren't a plumber, you're likely to end up in this category unless you already have a job lined up before moving. Pay will be in the $12--$15/hr range[95].

Don't put too big an emphasis on your educational background when looking for a job, unless it's relevant, as broadly defined. If you're an engineer, you might land an engineering job or you might end up at Home Depot, but the engineering degree will give you hiring

---

95   Keep in mind that Hawai'i has a very high percentage of the population with health care. Even part-time workers are entitled to full benefits.

preference in the Home Depot hardware department over someone without a technical education. If you have a degree in Medieval French Literature, you will be competing for cleaning jobs against middle-aged ladies with experience[96]. Good luck.

There are exceptions, of course. If you're a specialist in high rise construction, you might well find good work in your field in Honolulu, which as more high rise buildings per square anything than most other places on earth. You most definitely won't find it on Maui, where a high rise is a building with stairs. Do the footwork.

There is another quirk about the Hawai'i economy that bears mention. For some reason, it encourages entrepreneurs. Even at the level of mendicant, it shows up in street people with signs offering to recycle plastic, glass, and metal containers (and keep the deposit). Yard men will go to the door of newly-occupied houses and offer their services. People with fruit trees in their yard will set up a fruit stand for a few weeks while mangos are in season. Hawai'i must have the highest density of entrepreneurs, albeit on a sometimes small scale, outside of Silicon Valley.

Speaking of, if you are able to telecommute, or whatever you do is done on-line, you're in luck. Internet service is widely available and fast, and the time difference gives you something of an edge. For example, if your client e-mails you at 4 o'clock that they need something by the start of business the next morning, you've got at least a 3-hour edge on the west coast in which to get your work done and not stay up late. Late

---

96   Of course, that's true on the mainland, too.

night instructions/requests/badgering comes to you in the afternoon, while you have time to deal with it. I personally find this very helpful; people with constantly changing instructions and requests generally give up in the afternoon, my time, leaving me plenty of time to deal with it, uninterrupted. On the down side, an 8 am teleconference, New York time, is at the brutal hour of 2 am Hawaiian time, so that's not so good. Of course, you can telecommute from bed, too, and you don't need to dress up for the occasion.

Everybody does something, has some kind of work, even the seriously retired; it alleviates whatever issues might arise from being on a small island in the middle of a big ocean, it provides economic support, and it's expected in a subconscious way. We know an 84-year-old man who raises pineapples in his yard for fun and profit. It is not unusual for younger people to work 2 or 3 jobs, especially if they're in category 3 above, and it seems as though every third person is somehow in the property management or caretaking business. Curiously, the people who have advanced degrees and clean rental houses or stock shelves at Home Depot aren't resentful about it; they seem to view it as a vacation job, something they do voluntarily.

This is a hard concept to convey[97], but true. The lady who delivers the drinks to the golfers in her little cart is generally happier than the golfers on vacation. It's about the attitude. For one thing, the lady in the cart goes home in Hawai'i at the end of the day, and might stop at the beach to watch the sunset or take a dip on the

---

97   Right in there with "don't bring your down jacket to Hawai'i" hard.

way; how bad can that be? While the visiting golfers will eventually have to go back to snow or something equally not-fun.

So, a lot of the employment is nominally menial labor, serving visitors. Unless you fit in category 1 or 2 above, or have entrepreneurial blood, those are the jobs.

Four Years Later

After living here for a while, a little update seems in order, so I've tweaked this section a few times. Are we still as enthralled as we were at first? Do we have any other observations or advice? Yes to both.

Nice Guy to Butthead Ratio

Hawai'i has about the highest ratio of nice guys to buttheads of any place I've ever been, including Disneyland[98]. There are, of course, annoying teenagers, grumpy clerks, people with bad parking habits, and people just having a bad day, but they are rare; much more so than I would expect. Public employees are generally

---

98 Not the happiest place on earth, and more expensive than Hawai'i.

helpful[99], the trash guys (ours are Erick and Josh) go out of there way to get all the trash, drivers of slow-moving vehicles pull over, and nobody cuts in line.

You will still meet the occasional person who doesn't want you around. This happens; I've met people pretty much everywhere who didn't want me there, wherever "there" was. It makes a difference if you arrive gently; quietly, without a rush. It takes a while for newcomers to integrate, which helps explain why so many leave. Generally speaking, people are nice, and it's contagious.

Expensive? Sort-of.

I have a friend who swears it's cheaper to live in Hawai'i than where he came from, Sacramento. He says that what with the much lower property tax for residents, lower income tax for non-rich people, low sales tax, and lack of need for heating and to some extent, cooling, his savings offset the higher cost of gasoline, food, and anything imported. Maybe, compared to Sacramento. Compared to, for instance, Nebraska, it's probably higher. Property certainly costs more than, say, Detroit.

Personally, we notice higher grocery costs, partly offset by prudent bulk buying at Costco and shopping local producers; and a substantial markup on home improvement supplies[100]. On the other hand, we spend effectively nothing on entertainment, heating and cooling. Health care expenses are significant for non-Medicare,

---

99   Including, amazingly, at the Motor Vehicle office.

100   Now well into the fifth year of a seemingly-forever remodeling project, so we notice that.

non-employed persons; a part time job could probably fix that; 20 hours a week gets health coverage here. Moving from Albuquerque, overall costs for everything may be slightly higher. An oil change, for instance, is about $50.

We do quite a bit of on-line shopping; Amazon Prime is well worth the modest cost to join, and with a Firestick, we get free movies too. Watch out for shipping costs from other vendors; some seem to think the only way to ship is next day air. USPS Priority mail is your friend, but avoid parcel post; it can take, literally, months.

One thing that is much more expensive is property. Property values are well past the bottom of the market, rising from the 2008-2010 low at about 1% a month. Right now, home prices where we live, on the west side of Hawai'i Island in a semi-resort community, are about double what they were per square foot in Albuquerque. On the other hand, we spend much more time outside than we ever did, so we manage just fine with less square footage.

We recently replaced our from-the-mainland vehicle with a new car. We approached this with dread; most of the local dealers look at us like a cat views a can of sardines. Much to our surprise, we learned that inter-island car shopping was easy. We e-mailed every dealer of our chosen brand in the state asking for their price on a specific inventory vehicle; two bothered to reply, and we went with the dealer on Maui, who offered a great price and was very helpful. Shipping a 6000 lb truck from Maui to Hawai'i Island via barge took 4 days and cost a bit over $500; it's done all the time.

One thing that is shockingly expensive is travel to and from the islands. We have had exactly three visits

by mainland friends, and one of them was accidental[101].
This results in isolation from former friends and family
unless they're independently wealthy; and when and if
they do come, they will wear you out[102]. Let go of any
ideas of visiting relatives two or three times a year, it's
just too expensive and too hard a trip[103].

It's Not Just an Endless Vacation

We have a house to maintain, work, sort-of, to do,
and all the normal maintenance things, just like any other middle-class kind-of retired people. We do not spend
18 hours a day at the beach and the other 6 wishing we
were. Well, that last part is true. We generally go swimming, snorkeling, outrigger canoeing, sightseeing, and
other vacation-like activities two or three times a week.
The rest of the time is spent working around the house,
working on work-like things, making the seemingly-
endless supply runs to Costco, and general maintenance
activities like everybody else.

Since we live in a normal house in a normal neighborhood, not in a ritzy vacation resort or condo with every
possible maintenance need fulfilled, restaurants in abundance, and a golf course nearly at the front door, our lives
are much more like they were on the mainland in the
sense of daily activities. It's not the "endless summer"
you might imagine or wish for. You can have that, or

---

101 She actually came to visit someone else, so it shouldn't count.

102 Since it is so expensive, visitors want to pack in as much as they can in
their time here. I'm exhausted thinking about it.

103 Five and a half hours from LAX to Honolulu, then a short trip to Kona.
Rough.

something like it, if you are willing to pay condo mainte-nance fees, handyman fees, and assorted other expenses. Get ready for some serious money to change hands.

On the other hand, we can, when we want to, go to the beach with about 5 minutes preparation and 20 minutes travel time, at virtually no expense, any time we want. That's pretty good.

Medical Care?

Here on the Big Island, doctors are a little sparse, but some kind of medical coverage is nearly universal in Hawai'i so they've figured out how to make things work. At present there are only two significant health care insurers in Hawai'i; Kaiser Permanente and Hawai'i Medical Services Association (HMSA).

The unemployed, formerly non-Medicare member of our family paid for HMO coverage through Kaiser Permanente. It was a little less expensive, and with a low-er co-pay, than comparable coverage was on the main-land. In fact, with the advent of the Affordable Care Act, the rates went down, and coverage got better. Medicare persons pay a slightly higher co-pay ($15 office visit) for 5-star[104] Medicare coverage. Kaiser Permanente has a centralized-care model; urgent care and many outpatient procedures are done in local clinics, but specialist care is centralized in Honolulu, and patients and caretakers are flown there on regular carriers and housed in Honolulu if necessary. Some specialists visit clinics here on a periodic basis as well.

---

104 The Medicare system's highest rating for care. Pretty good! I had to change this footnote; the hospital food is actually excellent.

The other major health care network, HMSA, is a PPO, rather than HMO, model. Participants can use any provider who belongs to the network, but the choice can be very limited on the neighbor islands because of the small population and rural environment. Costs are comparable.

Urgent events such as cardiac arrests, traffic accidents, etc are probably a little harder to manage quickly simply because the island is so big and spread out. We have had occasions to test this and the paramedics arrived in 5 minutes, ready to go to work, which is pretty good. Here, the sparse traffic and good roads might actually be a help. Plus, bigger and better equipped facilities are only a brief 25 minute helicopter flight away on a neighboring island.

If one wants quick access to top-quality medical care to be a high priority, Hawai'i might not be the best choice. If medical care is important but not in the top half-dozen reasons to pick a place to live, it'll do fine.

Food

Hawai'i is a net importer of food, mostly from the same places as the mainland US; The Philippines and Central America. This is somewhat surprising, because the soil is good and water is plentiful, and at one time Hawai'i supported a sizeable population and was a food exporter. It's just that the low labor cost in some other places offsets the added burden of shipping. Nonetheless, there is a movement to achieve "food sovereignty"; to raise enough food that imports are no longer necessary.

Local produce is quite good, and some restaurants

feature a "farm to table" approach, with produce and vegetables raised on their own or contract farms for their use. Restaurants on O'ahu in particular promote "Big Island" meat and vegetables as premium items. In fact, local fruit and vegetables can be astonishingly good, and reasonable in price.

As you might expect, fish is a dietary staple, and it can be excellent. The cost is a bit lower than the mainland (no surprise there), but not a lot. What you get, is fresh fish. Really fresh.

Locally-raised beef[105] is a sought-after gourmet item in some places. We get ours at a local store, about $6/lb for rib steak. Bear in mind that it's grass fed and so tastes different from corn fed, and is from pretty muscular cattle. Lamb is a little pricy, probably because it's a boutique product, processed by small operations. For some reason, there doesn't seem to be much in the way of local poultry raising on a commercial scale, although rural people all seem to have chickens[106].

Pretty much anything that likes sunlight and water will grow, unless it wants a hard freeze or a short winter day. Apples, peaches, and the like simply do not grow, the weather is too uniform, as is the length of the day. Anything tropical, however, thrives, as do most vegetables[107]. Many people have mango, papaya, or citrus trees in their yards, and they are excellent. Bananas grow like weeds.

---

105 Parker Ranch on the Big Island is the second largest cattle ranch in the US. Really.

106 That's in addition to the feral chickens, which are all over the islands. Wild turkeys, too.

107 Carrots are hard to grow; the soil can be pretty hard and carrots have a tough time penetrating it.

Entertainment

We don't get a lot of touring Broadway shows, rock concerts, and the like. We occasionally get performances in off-beat places by world-class entertainers, possibly because they either live here or have friends.

We get the same movies and TV shows as the mainland, but a bit later. The time difference makes television interesting sometimes; one can find the winner of TV contests on the internet hours before the local broadcast.

We do have world-class hula (the annual *Merry Monarch Hula Festival,* which hosts competitors from around the world, is held in Hilo), ukelele, slack string guitar, and other Hawaiian and Polynesian entertainment. Some of these are not easily found anywhere else in the United States.

When we first moved here a total stranger told me that if one wasn't interested in water sports, he shouldn't bother moving to Hawai'i. He was partly right; one can fill lots of hours looking at, photographing, painting, and just admiring the scenery, but water activities are probably a prime reason for coming.

We swim, snorkel, and paddle outrigger canoes (as part of the local canoe club, which owns the canoes). We're working up to stand up paddle boarding, have rejected kayaking as not as much fun as outriggers, and haven't tried fishing yet. There're other possibilities, we're just not there.

The outrigger canoe thing is worth mentioning because it's such a part of the Hawaiian heritage. Canoe clubs are all over the place, with groups for all ages and abilities. No place but Hawai'i and Polynesia are canoes such an important part of the culture.

So pretty much, that's part of the trade-off; give up to some extent "canned" entertainment, shopping, etc. in return for seriously good outdoor activities, a terrific climate, and a generally nice place to live.

The Weather; is it Really That Good?

Yep. Mostly.

There's about a 5 degree difference in average winter and summer temperatures. In Kailua Kona the all-time record high was about 90F, and the all-time record low was about 65F. Those are records, not averages. Most of the time the temperature is between 70 and 80; warmer in the summer, but not by much.

Really bad weather such as hurricanes and tropical storms are rare events. Hurricane Iselle was the first to strike the Big Island in recorded history, in August of 2014. It did significant damage on the east side of the island, but stopped cold when it hit the two 14,000 ft mountains. Parts of the island were without power for many days because fallen trees made it difficult to restore the utilities. One person was killed by flooding.

There is also the ever-present possibility of a tsunami in coastal regions. Some coastal areas, including downtown Hilo, have been devastated by tsunamis in the past.

Generally, we can count on some level of sun every day, trade winds about 80% of the time, and depending on where one is standing, rain events ranging from every afternoon to a couple of times a year. We don't have snow (at least down here; it snows on Mauna Kea, though), hail, much in the way of thunderstorms, ice, freezing rain, tornados, or any of that other bad stuff that gets reported on TV.

Something to be aware of, though; the good climate means lots of bugs. We've gotten very friendly with our exterminator. And when the trade winds blow, there is dirt everywhere. You don't notice these things in a resort setting because they make sure you don't see them; but living here on a permanent basis means that you get to be very familiar with the many different species of insects that thrive in a tropical setting, and become accustomed to dirt and sand pretty much everywhere.

Company's Coming

Or maybe not. We originally thought, everybody wants to come visit, right? So we'll furnish a nice guest room, complete with queen-sized bed, night stands, closet space, etc. and plan on lots of company. Not so. It seems that since the cost of getting here is prohibitive, most people simply aren't going to visit. Some people do get frequent visitors, but it's not a certainty.

Instead, we've revised the guest room into another office, complete with sofa/hide-a-bed just in case, but the primary use will be office space, not waiting-for-company space.

The way it actually works is that most people, if they can afford to get here, can easily afford a place to stay, especially if we find it for them. If we had extra room they'd be glad to stay, but it's not necessary. We know of good deals at vacation rentals that can be had for much less than the going rate because we can make reservations a long time in advance, and because we're local and vouch for our company. So, we have a sofa/bed for casual company, such as a friend visiting from another island or a grandchild, and anybody else can stay in a rental that we'll find for a good price.

Cultural Shock

It may not be obvious to the resort-visitor or the new-comer just how much the Hawaiian culture is embedded in everyday Hawaiian life. I've mentioned the frequent and common use of Hawaiian words, but it bears repeating. Similarly, Hawaiian traditions are widely practiced and honored, even in minor things. It is normal to have prayers and chants before significant undertakings such as the launch of a canoe, the start of an athletic season, or the start of a construction project; in fact, just about any occasion for which there is an element of chance or risk and the favor of the Gods would be helpful.

Hawai'i is a relatively small group of small islands, inhabited for a really long time and without much in the way of natural processes to disturb man-made ar-tifacts. Consequently, Hawaiian relics of various kinds abound; stone walls, fire pits, structures, fish ponds; they're all over the place. Any construction has to be sensitive to these artifacts, so building gets done slowly. Some things, such as burials and Hawaiian temples, are generally *kapu* (forbidden) and should just plain be left alone. The newcomer needs to ignore his

National Geographic -inspired instincts to investigate these quaint native artifacts. You wouldn't desecrate a church, would you?

Would I do it Again?
Of course. But there are things I'd do differently.

- I'd ship both cars that we had on the mainland. The increased value here is much more than the shipping cost.

- I'd re-think what I bring if I knew then what I know now. Generally, if it's worth more than shipping cost, I'd bring it (clothing excepted.) If nothing else, I could get top dollar for it here.

- I would not, for sure, bring fancy suits, down clothing, or even many shoes. Not worth the shipping cost.

- I'd rent for a while before buying, if possible. We didn't have that luxury, being saddled with two dogs and a cat.

- Speaking of which, seriously consider how attached you really are to pets. If you just put up with them, save yourself some grief and considerable expense and find them new homes.

- I'd subscribe to the local paper, no matter what the cost, for several months before moving. Invaluable for getting a feel for the place and finding things like housing.

- I'd go with a local bank for a mortgage. None of the big mainland banks have offices here and the service is not so good. The local banks want my business and are willing to work with me. Interest rates are comparable and the service is so much better. Plus, when was the last time your mortgage holder gave you a hug?

See you at the beach. Or Costco.

Aloha!

This is Dennis. He lives in Hawi, and can teach you to play the ukelele. I promised I'd put him in my book.

Planning Calendar

1 Year

Visit island(s)
Subscribe to local newspaper
Begin sorting possessions
First round, pet vaccinations
Research and plan moving & shipping

6 Months

Visit again-seasonal differences
Meet with real estate people,
look at homes, rentals,, tentatively choose landing spot
FAVN tests for pets
Lock in housing
Reserve movers, container rental, etc.
Pet vaccinations
Rent PO Box
Arrange vehicle shipping
Book flights, rental car
Keep sorting! Lots of stuff to charity

1 Month

Begin address changes
Confirm housing

10 days (or less)

Final pet health exams

Index

Key to Photos

Welcome to Paradise

Welcome to Paradise

Welcome to Paradise

Dear Reader

If this was helpful, I'd like to hear about it, and I'd like you to share it. Authors, especially independent ones like me, depend on reviews. Please help me by leaving a review!

If it wasn't helpful, or if you have suggestions, I'd like to hear about that, too. Or, if you're thinking about a move and have questions, feel free to ask. In any event, you can reach me at *www.imagesbysam.com*, and see some of my photos as well.

Mahalo.

Welcome to Paradise

Made in the USA
Columbia, SC
16 December 2020

28208306R00075